S. Hrg. 112–652

IMPLEMENTATION OF THE NEW START TREATY, AND RELATED MATTERS

HEARING

BEFORE THE

COMMITTEE ON FOREIGN RELATIONS
UNITED STATES SENATE

ONE HUNDRED TWELFTH CONGRESS

SECOND SESSION

JUNE 21, 2012

Printed for the use of the Committee on Foreign Relations

Available via the World Wide Web: http://www.gpo.gov/fdsys/

U.S. GOVERNMENT PRINTING OFFICE

77–373 PDF   WASHINGTON : 2012

For sale by the Superintendent of Documents, U.S. Government Printing Office
Internet: bookstore.gpo.gov Phone: toll free (866) 512–1800; DC area (202) 512–1800
Fax: (202) 512–2104 Mail: Stop IDCC, Washington, DC 20402–0001

(II)

CONTENTS

(III)

IMPLEMENTATION OF THE NEW START TREATY, AND RELATED MATTERS

THURSDAY, JUNE 21, 2012

U.S. SENATE,
COMMITTEE ON FOREIGN RELATIONS,
Washington, DC.

The committee met, pursuant to notice, at 10:05 a.m., in room SD–419, Dirksen Senate Office Building, Hon. John F. Kerry (chairman of the committee) presiding.

Present: Senators Kerry, Shaheen, Udall, Lugar, Corker, Risch, and Isakson.

OPENING STATEMENT OF HON. JOHN F. KERRY, U.S. SENATOR FROM MASSACHUSETTS

The CHAIRMAN. The hearing will come to order.

Thank you all very much. We are running a couple of minutes late because we had Russia PNTR down in the Finance Committee, and we are moving under the cloud of a U.S. Senate vote-a-thon, which will begin again at 11 a.m. The last few days have been super voting, I guess.

So we are going to try, and we don't have that many Senators here yet. We will see how many come. But my plan is to start with a 5-minute round, and then we can have a second round, if needed. But if fewer Senators show up, then we will expand that when the questioning time comes.

Obviously, evaluating the New START Treaty and debating its merits was a major undertaking here, and I am very grateful to Secretary Gottemoeller and to others who contributed to what I thought was a very extensive and productive effort to evaluate that treaty and to lay the groundwork to put a record together. We scrutinized it through months of open and classified hearings, hundreds of questions for the record, more than a week of debate in the full Senate.

And ultimately, the committee supported it 14 to 4, and we passed it in the full Senate with 71 votes. And I observed, along with a few others, that in today's Washington, 71 is probably the old 95. But regardless, I am proud that we sent a signal to the world that we remain committed to trying to reduce the threat of nuclear proliferation.

Now it has been almost a year and a half since the Senate agreed to the New START and just over a year since it entered into force. So it is appropriate at this juncture to review how well the treaty is performing.

We said we would do that, and we are doing it. And Senator Corker and Senator Isakson particularly made it clear that that was an important part of their willingness to be supportive, and we appreciate that and want to respect all of the commitments that were made with respect to the treaty. So it is important to me as chair and to Senator Lugar, who has spent a lifetime on this topic, that we do our due diligence.

So I look forward to hearing from our witnesses today. I just want to say a couple of quick things about it maybe to help frame the discussion a little bit. I think there is a very good story to be told.

First, the United States has already conducted 23 short-notice inspections of Russian nuclear weapons bases since the ratification. That is pretty significant. On 23 occasions, teams of well-trained, well-prepared U.S. inspectors have, on short notice, brought radiation scanners and other equipment to highly sensitive Russian nuclear bases of our choosing.

Now we depend on these short-notice inspections to verify that Russia has been telling us the truth about those facilities and the nuclear weapon systems that they house. Thanks to New START, we get to do these inspections 18 times a year for the next 10 years.

Second, the treaty gives us visibility into Russia's nuclear activities. Every 6 months, the United States receives a comprehensive database from Russia detailing where its strategic weapons systems are located and whether they are deployed, undergoing maintenance, or being retired.

And that database doesn't just sit there for 6 months. Between those 6-month updates, we receive hundreds of notifications from the Russians on the numbers, locations, and technical characteristics of weapons systems and facilities that are subject to the treaty's verification provisions.

These notifications allow us to track movements and changes in the status of Russia's nuclear arsenal. And what that means in practice is that we now have far more up-to-date information on each Russian missile, each launcher, each bomber than we had before we ratified the treaty.

Now despite the clear benefits to our security, there are some critics who nevertheless argue that somehow we did Russia a favor by ratifying New START. I think the facts just don't support that.

First of all, we didn't sign up to the New START Treaty as a favor to anybody, let alone Russia, and any more than 95 United States Senators in 2003 under President Bush were doing a favor for Russia when they voted to support the Bush administration's Strategic Offensive Reductions Treaty.

Talk to former Secretary of Defense Bob Gates. He certainly wasn't seeking to do a favor when he supported New START. Neither were the commanders of U.S. Strategic Command, the Chairman of the Joint Chiefs of Staff, or Condoleezza Rice, Steve Hadley, Brent Scowcroft, and Jim Schlesinger. The only question for them was whether the treaty benefited our national security. They thought it did, and as I said, 71 Senators agreed.

Now, frankly, those who say we should just walk away from New START—or who never supported it in the first place because of our differences with Russia—really have a fundamental responsibility which they have never fulfilled, which is explain to the American people how retaining more nuclear weapons than our military advisers say we need and how having less insight into Russia's strategic nuclear arsenal would change Russia's calculus toward Syria or its approach to human rights or any other issue. We need to see the logic of that.

Now, of course, when the Senate ratified New START, it also supported additional resources to maintain our own nuclear weapons infrastructure. And far from falling short on commitments, the administration has been working hard to provide increased support for the complex at a time when almost all other budgets are being slashed.

Last year, the President requested what he said he would under the 10-year plan to fund the nuclear weapons complex. It was the House of Representatives that cut the funding below the request—not the President. And this year, the President asked for another 5 percent increase for the budget over last year.

So, with that, I welcome our distinguished witnesses. Rose Gottemoeller, well known to the Senate, led the U.S. team that negotiated the treaty as the Assistant Secretary of State for Verification and Compliance. She is back today as the Acting Under Secretary of State for Arms Control and International Security.

Tom D'Agostino is the Administrator of the National Nuclear Security Administration and the Under Secretary of Energy for Nuclear Security, and he was also a familiar face around the Senate during the New START debate. And he will address the status, challenges, and plans for our nuclear weapons laboratories and other infrastructure.

Finally, Madelyn Creedon is Assistant Secretary of Defense for Global Security Affairs, where she oversees policy developments for U.S. nuclear forces and missile defenses. And she is well known for her service on the staff of the Armed Services Committee. We welcome her back.

So thank you all for being here today. We look forward to your testimony and the opportunity to review where we are with respect to START.

Senator Lugar.

OPENING STATEMENT OF HON. RICHARD G. LUGAR, U.S. SENATOR FROM INDIANA

Senator LUGAR. Well, thank you, Mr. Chairman.

Today, the committee meets to review the implementation of the New START Treaty and to engage in a broader examination of United States nuclear policy.

I thank the chairman for holding this hearing. I commend Senator Corker for his efforts on this issue. We welcome back to the committee Acting Under Secretary Rose Gottemoeller. We welcome to the committee for the first time Thomas D'Agostino, the Administrator of the National Nuclear Security Administration, and Madelyn Creedon, Assistant Secretary of Defense for Global Security Affairs.

The Foreign Relations Committee, as the chairman has pointed out, approved the New START Treaty on September 16, 2010, by a vote of 14 to 4, after acting on dozens of amendments to the resolution of ratification and considering answers to more than a thousand questions for the record submitted in 12 hearings and multiple briefings. The Senate approved the treaty by a vote of 71–26 on December 22, 2010, after considering and voting on almost 40 amendments on the floor to both the treaty and the resolution of ratification in 8 days of floor debate.

We should not fail to appreciate the importance of what was achieved in December 2010. The final result occurred because a coalition of Senators from both parties joined to bolster the twin pillars of American nuclear security—arms control and modernization.

The legislative process resulted not only in the approval of the treaty, but also a commitment to spend $185 billion over 10 years to modernize nuclear warheads and delivery systems. This was a rational policy outcome that bolstered U.S. national security.

In my judgment, both the New START agreement and the nuclear modernization commitments were justified, even without reference to each other. It was essential to continue limits on Russian strategic nuclear forces and to ensure transparent inspections. It also was essential the United States adopt a plan for badly needed updates of our nuclear infrastructure and arsenal.

In other words, joining these two policies was not merely a marriage of convenience or a case of legislative log rolling. Both were good policies made even stronger by being accepted in the same political and policy context.

The outcome of the New START and nuclear modernization debate also represented an expression of unity and clarity in an area of national security policy where these attributes are key contributors to success. Nuclear policy is not an inconsequential seminar topic where players can score political points without incurring negative policy ramifications. Every aspect of our nuclear policy and the accompanying debates are scrutinized by the Russians, the Chinese, our allies, even rogue states.

This does not preclude vigorous debate. But in the end, we should attempt to reach consensus because it is good for U.S. national security to do so. At the very least, we must project a unified purpose.

The New START Treaty approval, accompanied by nuclear modernization commitments, established a solid basis for strategic nuclear policy for a decade going forward. It provided clarity to allies regarding the U.S. nuclear umbrella. It ensured the potency of our nuclear deterrent. It achieved transparency with respect to Russia's nuclear programs, and it was a foundation upon which talks with Russia on tactical nuclear weapons could be based.

The debate was not an easy one, but the outcome established a credible, broad-based plan for nuclear policy going forward. Like Senator Corker, I was among those who sought and obtained multiple assurances relating to the triad of American land, air, and sea-based strategic forces to ensure sufficient support in the Senate for the New START Treaty.

I am deeply concerned about the state of nuclear planning and programming within the Defense Department and the services regarding the triad. I am also very concerned by attempts to force

U.S. withdrawal from the New START Treaty or suspend its implementation. We should not risk either the transparency achieved by the treaty nor the reliability and performance of our strategic nuclear forces. Our goal should be to ensure robust implementation of New START, while reaffirming and funding commitments on modernization.

With regard to nuclear weapons, more broadly, it is my understanding the administration may soon complete its implementation study for the 2010 Nuclear Posture Review. Stories have appeared in the media that the administration is considering levels of nuclear weapons lower than those in article II of the New START Treaty. I hope our witnesses can clarify the President's position.

I simply would say that our country is strongest and our diplomacy is most effective when nuclear policy is made by deliberate decisions in which both the legislative and executive branches fully participate. This process should begin with the President of the United States. As the Chief Executive and Commander in Chief, he needs to engage with Congress on this topic personally, and he needs to weigh in more heavily on nuclear funding decisions.

Last, I would note that the Nunn-Lugar umbrella agreement with Russia expires next year. I would appreciate an update regarding the status of our negotiations with Russia on the umbrella agreement.

I look forward to the testimony of our witnesses, and I thank you, Mr. Chairman.

The CHAIRMAN. Thanks very much, Senator Lugar. Appreciate it.

I am going to reserve my time for questions, I just want to give you a heads-up. So that I am going to begin with Senator Lugar. We will go to Senator Udall, then Senator Corker, so that we can expedite here.

And if everybody could summarize their testimony in approximately 5 minutes, we would appreciate it. Full testimonies will be placed in the record as if delivered in full.

We will begin with Secretary Gottemoeller, then Secretary D'Agostino and Creedon. Thank you.

STATEMENT OF HON. ROSE GOTTEMOELLER, ACTING UNDER SECRETARY FOR ARMS CONTROL AND INTERNATIONAL SECURITY, U.S. DEPARTMENT OF STATE, WASHINGTON, DC

Ms. GOTTEMOELLER. Thank you very much, Mr. Chairman.

Thank you, Senator Lugar.

Senators, it is my pleasure and my honor to be here today again before the Senate Foreign Relations Committee with an opportunity to provide you an update on the implementation of the treaty between the United States of America and the Russian Federation on Measures for the Further Reduction and Limitation of Strategic Offensive Arms, or the New START Treaty.

It is a pleasure to be here today also with my colleagues from the interagency, with Tom D'Agostino of the DOE National Nuclear Security Administration and Madelyn Creedon of the Office of the Secretary of Defense. I think it is a good sign of the very solid working relationship that we have had in the interagency, both in the negotiation of this treaty and now in its implementation.

As you know, New START celebrated its first birthday this past February. Senator Kerry just referred to that. Its ratification and entry into force would not have been possible without the strong bipartisan support of this body. We are grateful to Senators on both sides of the aisle for supporting a treaty that has done so much to strengthen global and national security.

When the treaty is fully implemented, it will result in the lowest number of deployed nuclear warheads since the 1950s, the first full decade of the nuclear age—1,550 warheads deployed on or counted on 700 delivery vehicles, that is, intercontinental ballistic missiles, submarine-launched ballistic missiles, and bombers.

To illustrate the great distance we have traveled in reducing our nuclear weapons, I would like to mention that when the START Treaty was signed in July 1991, the United States and the U.S.S.R. had at that time each deployed approximately 10,550 nuclear warheads.

The current implementation process is providing ongoing transparency and predictability regarding the world's two largest deployed nuclear arsenals, while preserving our ability to maintain the strong nuclear deterrent that remains an essential element of U.S. national security and the security of our allies and friends.

To date, the implementation process has been very positive and pragmatic. Under New START, we are continuing the professional working relationship that was established with our Russian counterparts during the negotiation process in Geneva.

In the first treaty year, the United States and Russian Federation kept pace with each other in conducting inspections. Both parties conducted the yearly maximum of 18 inspections. So far during this treaty year, the Russian Federation has conducted eight inspections and the United States has conducted seven inspections. Therefore, Chairman, I have to update you a bit. We are now up to 25 short-notice inspections since the treaty entered into force.

These inspections have taken place on intercontinental ballistic missiles, submarine-launched ballistic missiles, and heavy bombers at their operating bases; storage facilities; conversion or elimination facilities; and test ranges.

Through inspection activities, we have acquired new and valuable information. For example, New START includes intrusive reentry vehicle inspections that are designed to confirm the exact number of reentry vehicles, or warheads, on individual missiles selected for inspection. We are now able to confirm the exact number of warheads on any randomly selected Russian ICBM and SLBM, something that we were not able to do under the 1991 START Treaty.

Another aspect of treaty implementation is the exhibition process. These exhibitions provide both parties with an opportunity to see new types of strategic offensive arms, view distinguishing features, and confirm declared data.

Both sides have conducted delivery vehicle exhibitions. In March 2010, the United States conducted exhibitions of its B–1B and B–2A heavy bombers. Following that, the Russian Federation conducted exhibitions of its RS–24 ICBM and associated mobile launcher.

That was the first time we had a chance to see the RS–24—the new Russian mobile missile—and its launch vehicle. This exhibition provided us with a great amount of information that we would not otherwise have had.

The United States and the Russian Federation have also been sharing a veritable mountain of data with each other. The chairman mentioned the notification process. At this point, since entry into force, we have exchanged over 2,500 notifications through our Nuclear Risk Reduction Centers.

They help to track the movement and changes in the status of systems on a day-in, day-out basis. That, combined with the databases that we exchange every 6 months, gives us an opportunity to have a kind of living database, a truly real-time look at what is going on inside the Russian strategic forces.

I will draw my remarks to a close at this point, but I just want to underscore that our experience so far is demonstrating that the New START's verification regime works and will help to push open the door to new and more complicated verification techniques in the future. We look forward to reporting on further success in the implementation of this treaty, and I thank you for the opportunity to make these remarks to you today.

Thank you very much.

[The prepared statement of Ms. Gottemoeller follows:]

PREPARED STATEMENT OF ACTING UNDER SECRETARY OF STATE ROSE GOTTEMOELLER

Mr. Chairman, Senator Lugar, and members of the Foreign Relations Committee, thank you for this opportunity to provide an update on the implementation of the treaty between the United States of America and the Russian Federation on Measures for the Further Reduction and Limitation of Strategic Offensive Arms (New START).

As you know, New START celebrated its first birthday this past February. Its ratification and entry into force would not have been possible without the strong bipartisan support of this body. We are grateful to Senators on both sides of the aisle for supporting a treaty that has done so much to strengthen global and national security.

When the treaty is fully implemented, it will result in the lowest number of deployed nuclear warheads since the 1950s, the first full decade of the nuclear age: 1,550 warheads deployed on 700 delivery vehicles, that is, intercontinental ballistic missiles, submarine-launched ballistic missiles, and bombers.[1] To illustrate the great distance we have traveled in reducing our nuclear weapons, I would like to mention that when the START Treaty was signed in July 1991, the United States and the former Union of Soviet Socialist Republics (USSR) each deployed approximately 10,500 nuclear warheads.

The current implementation process is providing ongoing transparency and predictability regarding the world's two largest deployed nuclear arsenals, while preserving our ability to maintain the strong nuclear deterrent that remains an essential element of U.S. national security and the security of our allies and friends.

The verification regime for New START is a detailed and extensive set of data exchanges and timely notifications covering all strategic offensive arms and facilities covered by the treaty, as well as onsite inspections, exhibitions, restrictions on where specified items may be located, and additional transparency measures.

In negotiating the treaty, both sides worked hard to find innovative new mechanisms to aid in the verification of the treaty and the results of that work are already evident. The regime provides for effective verification and, at the same time, is simpler to implement and lessens disruptions to the day-to-day operations of both sides' strategic forces.

---

[1] The treaty's central limits are as follows: 700 deployed ICBMs, deployed SLBMs and deployed heavy bombers; 1,550 warheads on deployed ICBMs and SLBMs and nuclear warheads counted for deployed heavy bombers; and 800 deployed and nondeployed ICBM launchers, SLBM launchers, and heavy bombers.

These verification mechanisms are enabling us to monitor and inspect Russia's strategic nuclear forces to ensure compliance with the provisions of the treaty. For both the United States and Russia, accurate and timely knowledge of each other's nuclear forces helps to prevent the risks of misunderstandings, mistrust, and worst-case analysis and policymaking.

To date, the implementation process has been positive and pragmatic. Under New START, we are continuing the professional working relationship that was established during the negotiation process in Geneva.

In the first treaty year, the United States and the Russian Federation kept pace with each other on conducting inspections. Both Parties conducted the yearly maximum of 18 inspections. So far this treaty year, the Russian Federation has conducted 8 inspections and the United States has conducted 6 inspections. These inspections have taken place at intercontinental ballistic missile (ICBM), submarine-launched ballistic missile (SLBM), and heavy bomber bases; storage facilities; conversion or elimination facilities; and test ranges.

Through inspection activities, we have acquired new and valuable information. For example, New START includes intrusive reentry vehicle inspections that are designed to confirm the exact number of reentry vehicles (or warheads) on individual missiles selected for inspection. We are now able to confirm the actual number of warheads on any randomly selected Russian ICBM and SLBM—something we were not able to do under the 1991 Strategic Arms Reduction Treaty (START).

Another new feature in the New START is that each ICBM, SLBM, and heavy bomber has been assigned a unique identifier (UIDs)—a license plate, if you will. These UIDs are helping both sides with a "cradle to grave" tracking of the location and status of strategic offensive arms from arrival at an operating base, movement between facilities, changes in deployment status, maintenance or storage, to eventual conversion or elimination.

Another aspect of treaty implementation is the exhibition process. The purpose of exhibitions is to demonstrate distinguishing features, to confirm technical characteristics of new types, and to demonstrate the results of conversion of the first item of each type of strategic offensive arms subject to this treaty. These exhibitions provide both Parties with an opportunity to see new types of strategic offensive arms, view distinguishing features, and confirm declared data. These exhibitions assist in the conduct of onsite inspections. They also serve to enhance transparency and provide a better understanding of each other's systems.

Both sides have conducted delivery vehicle exhibitions. In March 2011, the United States conducted exhibitions of its B–1B and B–2A heavy bombers. Following that, the Russian Federation conducted exhibitions of its RS–24 ICBM and associated mobile launcher. That was the first time we had a chance to see the RS–24, the new Russian mobile missile with multiple warheads. This exhibition provided us with a great amount of information we would have not otherwise had.

In March 2012, the United States conducted the first of four one-time cruise missile submarine (SSGN) exhibitions. The purpose of these exhibitions is to confirm that the launchers on these submarines are incapable of launching SLBMs.

The United States and the Russian Federation have also been sharing a veritable mountain of data with each other. Since entry into force, we have exchanged over 2,500 notifications through our Nuclear Risk Reduction Centers (NRRC). These notifications help to track movement and changes in the status of systems. For example, a notification is sent every time a heavy bomber is moved out of its home base for more than 24 hours. Additionally, when the United States conducts a flight test of an ICBM or SLBM, the NRRC will notify the Russian National Center 1 day in advance of the flight test. The Russians provide the same information for their launches. Our center receives from the Russian NRRC the incoming notification via our secure government-to-government communications link. We translate it, make secure telephonic alerts, and issue a State Department cable to concerned U.S. agencies within 1 hour.

On top of the individual notifications, we exchange a comprehensive database of strategic forces covered by the treaty every 6 months. This full account combines with the notifications to create a living, growing document that continuously tracks each side's strategic nuclear forces.

These data exchanges are providing us with an even more detailed picture of Russian strategic forces than we were able to obtain from earlier exchanges and the inspections allow us to confirm the validity of that data. Of course, the verification regime is backed up by our own National Technical Means of verification, our satellites and other monitoring platforms.

Another feature of the New START Treaty implementation process is the Bilateral Consultative Commission (BCC). This compliance and implementation body has met three times since entry into force. The BCC has produced Joint Statements and

9

agreements, memorializing shared understandings of technical issues related to implementation activities. As in the implementation of the treaty overall the environment in the BCC has been one of practical problem-solving on both sides of the table.

The latest session of the BCC was held in Geneva from January 24 to February 7, 2012. During the session, both sides continued their discussion on practical issues related to the implementation of the treaty. The United States and the Russian Federation reached agreement there on an outstanding issue from the negotiations— the exchange of telemetric information on an agreed number of ICBM and SLBM launches and the procedures for conducting demonstrations of recording media and/ or telemetric information playback equipment. Since this agreement, both the United States and the Russian Federation have conducted demonstrations of telemetric information playback equipment and recording media to be used during telemetry exchanges. Telemetric information was exchanged between the Parties on April 6, 2012.

Our experience so far is demonstrating that the New START's verification regime works, and will help to push the door open to new, more complicated verification techniques for the future. Verification will be crucial to any future nuclear reduction plans and the United States has made it clear that we are committed to continuing a step-by-step process to reduce the overall number of nuclear weapons.

Further, the outstanding working relationship that developed during the negotiations has carried over into the implementation phase, creating an atmosphere of bilateral cooperation to resolve implementation questions as they have arisen. We look forward to reporting further success and additional updates as New START implementation progresses.

Thank you again for the opportunity to speak and I look forward to your questions.

The CHAIRMAN. Thanks, Secretary Gottemoeller.

Secretary D'Agostino.

STATEMENT OF HON. THOMAS P. D'AGOSTINO, ADMINISTRATOR OF THE NATIONAL NUCLEAR SECURITY ADMINISTRATION AND UNDER SECRETARY FOR NUCLEAR SECURITY, U.S. DEPARTMENT OF ENERGY, WASHINGTON, DC

Mr. D'AGOSTINO. Chairman Kerry, Ranking Member Lugar, members of the committee, thank you very much for the opportunity to testify today concerning the implementation of the New START Treaty, the nuclear deterrent, and the future of our nuclear security enterprise.

I want to thank the chair and ranking for their continued bipartisan leadership on nuclear security issues in the U.S. Congress. In particular, I would like to recognize Ranking Member Lugar for his distinguished career as a champion for nuclear nonproliferation policy.

Senator Lugar, your leadership on treaty negotiations and verification, thoughtful and measured diplomacy, and efforts to reduce the threat of nuclear, chemical, and biological weapons are unique in both the U.S. Senate and American history.

The Nunn-Lugar Cooperative Threat Reduction Program has led to the implementation of the most significant security measures since the end of the cold war, and it continues to be a real force in preventing terrorism. I sincerely hope that your voice continues to remain a major part of our future policy discussions.

Thank you, sir.

Working closely with our colleagues at the Department of State and Department of Defense, the National Nuclear Security Administration has played an essential role in the New START Treaty negotiations and continues to contribute directly to successful implementation of the treaty. With entry into force, we continue to support inspection implementation matters within the United States.

This has included our work with the United States interagency and sites across the nuclear security enterprise to review and assess Russian Federation radiation detection equipment for use during inspections in the United States. Through Sandia National Laboratories, we are conducting technical analyses and support on inspection matters.

The extensive notifications, inspections, and exchange of telemetric information required by the treaty have provided the tools the United States and the Russian Federation require, ensuring transparency and predictability regarding each other's strategic nuclear forces. This allows us to plan future stockpile and infrastructure requirements with increased confidence.

And the President's commitment in this area and to the obligations of the New START is evident. NNSA has seen consistent support since he took office in 2009. In fiscal year 2013, if the 2013 appropriations and authorizations comes through, this will result in a close to 20 percent increase in our program in the past few years, and this is unprecedented.

The administration and Congress recognized the need to sustain our nuclear weapons in the stockpile and to modernize the infrastructure and the people capabilities of the enterprise to ensure our stockpile remains safe, secure, and effective. We are extending the life of approximately 80 percent of our active stockpile to ensure that it remains a viable and credible deterrent for decades to come.

Four weapons systems—the W76, the B61, the W78, and W88— are currently beyond the Phase 6.1 process in life extensions. We are in production with the W76–1. We are about to transition to development engineering on the B61 warhead, and we have commenced life extension feasibility studies for the W78 and the W88.

As you are all aware, the administration is making these investments at a time of great fiscal pressure. Between the Budget Control Act passed by Congress, the four life extension programs I previously mentioned, and our aging infrastructure, hard choices have had to be made. And we are continuously assessing our scope of work with the Defense Department, challenging our people to drive efficiencies.

However, the investments continue. And just this week, a key piece of the Chemistry and Metallurgy Research Replacement Facility opened at Los Alamos National Laboratory. The radiological laboratory and office building will play a key role implementing the United States plutonium strategy, allowing us to maintain our world-class plutonium capabilities when we complete the program operations in the old existing CMR.

We also identified an important synergy with our plutonium disposition mission in South Carolina and can support both feedstock production for MOX plant and sustained expertise at Los Alamos in the existing plutonium facility No. 4.

Our next major investment in the future of our enterprise and deterrent is the Uranium Processing Facility in Oak Ridge, TN. The Nation has no other option for maintaining highly enriched uranium processing capabilities in existing facilities. There are no other options.

We are replacing these required capabilities in order to maintain our deterrent and fuel our Navy submarines and aircraft carriers. We have also broken ground on the High Explosives Pressing Facility at Pantex to ensure the continuity for our life extension work, taking care of our stockpile.

NNSA continues to work closely with our partners at the Department of Defense to ensure the proper balance of resources and requirements, and we are continuing this work throughout the summer. This includes all of the programs that I have mentioned earlier.

Our budget request includes the funding necessary for research, development, test, and assessment of advanced monitoring and assessment capabilities. And looking ahead, we stand ready to support future treaty negotiations and development assessment processes.

Again, I thank you for the opportunity to be here today, and I look forward to your questions.

[The prepared statement of Mr. D'Agostino follows:]

PREPARED STATEMENT OF UNDER SECRETARY THOMAS P. D'AGOSTINO

Chairman Kerry, Ranking Member Lugar, and members of this committee, thank you for the opportunity to testify today about implementation of the New START Treaty, the nuclear deterrent, and the future of our nuclear security enterprise.

Before I begin, I want to thank the chair and ranking member for their continued bipartisan leadership on nuclear security issues in the U.S. Congress. In particular, I would like to recognize Ranking Member Lugar for his distinguished career as a champion for nuclear nonproliferation policy.

Senator Lugar, your leadership on treaty negotiations and verification, thoughtful and measured diplomacy, and efforts to reduce the threat of nuclear, chemical, and biological weapons are unique in both the U.S. Senate and American history. The Nunn-Lugar Cooperative Threat Reduction Program has led to some of the most significant security measures implemented since the end of the cold war, and has had a very real impact on preventing terrorism. Your leadership on these issues over the years will be sorely missed by everyone working to make the world safer for our children and grandchildren. I will personally miss working with you, and I sincerely hope that your voice remains a major part of future policy discussions.

Working with our colleagues at the Departments of State and Defense, the NNSA played an essential role throughout New START Treaty negotiations, and continues to contribute very directly to successful implementation of the treaty.

NNSA experts led negotiations on behalf of the U.S. Government for the notifications regime under New START, which since entry-into-force of the treaty has resulted in the exchange of over 2,400 notifications on strategic forces matters between the United States and Russian Federation. Our experts also led negotiations for the exchange of telemetric information, and since entry-into-force have worked to ensure the successful commencement of this exchange. This included leading negotiations within the treaty's Bilateral Consultative Commission (BCC) to complete the first two BCC Agreements, which provided the necessary treaty-based framework to allow the exchange of telemetric information to begin. As a result, in April of this year the United States and Russia exchanged the first set of telemetric information on missile flight tests since expiration of the original START Treaty in 2009. NNSA also led the negotiations for the treaty's definitions, which are relied upon for the full range of treaty implementation matters.

In addition to leading three working groups during negotiations, we contributed significantly to several of the other elements of the treaty, including the development of the treaty's inspection regime. With entry-into-force, we have continued to support inspection implementation matters within the United States. This has included essential work with the U.S. Interagency and sites across the nuclear security enterprise to review and assess the Russian Federation's radiation detection equipment (RDE) for use during inspections in the United States. Through Sandia National Laboratories, we are also conducting technical analyses associated with RDE measurements, and are providing other technical support on inspection matters.

Through the New START Treaty's extensive notifications, inspections, and the exchange of telemetric information, the United States and Russian Federation once again have the tools in place to ensure transparency and predictability regarding each other's strategic nuclear forces. It is this predictability that is of the greatest benefit to us. It allows us to plan future stockpile size and infrastructure requirements with significantly greater confidence.

The President's commitment to the obligations codified as part of New START is evident: NNSA, and the weapons activities account in particular, has seen consistent support since he took office in 2009. The administration and the Congress recognized the need to sustain the nuclear weapons in the stockpile and modernize the infrastructure and capabilities of the nuclear security enterprise. This September we will mark 20 years since the end of underground testing, and, due to the investments we have made in science-based stockpile stewardship, we know more about how our weapons age and perform than ever before. I have said this in the past and will reiterate again now: our stockpile is safe, secure, and effective.

Right now, we are extending the life of approximately 80 percent of our active stockpile to ensure that it remains a viable, credible deterrent for decades to come. Four weapons systems—the W76, B61, W78, and W88—are currently beyond phase 6.1 in the life extension process. We are in production with the W76–1, we are about to transition to Development Engineering on the B61–12, and we have begun life extension Feasibility Studies on the W78 and W88.

As you are all aware, the administration is making these investments at a time of great fiscal pressure. Between the Budget Control Act, passed by this Congress; the four life extension programs I mentioned; and our aging infrastructure, which, contrary to some opinions, has many features other than replacing the Chemistry and Metallurgy Research (CMR) facility at Los Alamos, hard choices have had to be made. We looked at our scope of work, we have strongly challenged our people to do more with less without compromising safety or quality, and we have made tough decisions focused on the future. NNSA continues to work with our partners at the Department of Defense (DOD) to balance resources and requirements, and that commitment has not waivered despite many external pressures.

For example, just this week a key piece of the Chemistry and Metallurgy Research Replacement (CMRR) facility opened. The Radiological Laboratory, Utility, and Office Building (RLUOB) will play a key support role implementing the United States plutonium strategy, allowing us to maintain our world-class plutonium capabilities when we complete program operations in the aging CMR facility in approximately 2019. In addition, we will consider options for staging bulk quantities of plutonium needed for future program use in Nevada at the Device Assembly Facility; evaluate options to share material characterization workload between the PF–4 facility at LANL and Building 332 as a Hazard Category 2, Security Category 3 nuclear facility at Lawrence Livermore National Laboratory; and accelerate plans to process, package, and ship excess special nuclear material in PF–4 for disposition. We also identified an important synergy with our plutonium disposition mission in South Carolina and can support both feedstock production for the MOX fuel fabrication plant and sustain plutonium expertise for defense purposes by utilizing the PF–4 facility at Los Alamos. These actions allow NNSA to continue current plutonium operations for the national security enterprise while we work to define a longer term strategy that aligns capabilities and future stockpile needs.

Our next major investment in the future of our enterprise and the nuclear deterrent is the Uranium Processing Facility (UPF) in Oak Ridge, TN. The Nation does not have any options for maintaining highly enriched uranium processing capabilities in existing facilities. When looking at consequences and likelihood of infrastructure failures across the nuclear security enterprise, our greatest risk is the potential failure of Building 9212 at Y–12, originally built in 1952, which would directly impact our ability to modernize the stockpile. We must replace the required UPF capability if we are going to maintain our deterrent and fuel our Navy's submarines and aircraft carriers. UPF will allow us to move uranium capabilities out of the decaying building 9212 and to consolidate and modernize all other highly enriched uranium processing capabilities that are in Buildings 9215, 9998, and 9204–2E to provide safer and more efficient operations. We have also broken ground on a new High Explosive Pressing Facility at Pantex to ensure continuity of capability for planned Life Extension Program workload.

The Nuclear Weapons Council (NWC) has been an integral part of this process. It would be irresponsible to make such forward-looking decisions without first talking to our partners in the DOD. As part of that process, the NWC approved a number of critical schedule adjustments in March that include the W76, B61, W78, W88, and the CMRR and UPF.

Beyond that, NNSA and the Office of the Secretary of Defense's Cost Assessment and Program Evaluation (CAPE) team have an interagency group doing further analysis on balancing the resources and requirements for the nuclear security enterprise. The NNSA CAPE effort will inform the President's Budget Request for FY 2014, which is currently being formulated.

Our coordination with DOD via the NWC is significant and detailed. We're demonstrating infrastructure responsiveness by increasing neutron generator production for the W78 when needed to meet changing stockpile requirements. We're continuing to sustain and improve the stockpile by replacing gas transfer systems to improve component lifetime and weapon performance margin. And we're working with the Department of the Air Force on an Analysis of Alternatives for the future of nuclear-capable air delivered cruise missiles. Our decisions are not made in a vacuum, and any impact that NNSA's priorities may have on the stockpile are fully informed by our working relationship with the NWC.

Looking ahead, consistent with the President's nuclear security agenda, the results of the Nuclear Posture Review, and instructions from the Senate to pursue negotiations for nonstrategic nuclear weapons, NNSA stands ready to support future negotiations and is developing and assessing capabilities to enable potential future monitoring and verification initiatives. We need to do our homework now to prepare for the future in a responsible manner, so that the United States can achieve its arms control and nonproliferation objectives while continuing to ensure the safety and security of our nuclear weapons stockpile and the facilities across the Nuclear Security Enterprise.

Toward this end, NNSA's FY13 request includes funding to research, develop, test and assess advanced monitoring and verification capabilities, including collaborative initiatives with foreign partners. These include advanced radiation detection techniques to confirm the presence of nuclear weapons while protecting sensitive information, chain of custody capabilities to monitor and track weapons and key components, and capabilities to confirm nuclear weapons dismantlement and disposition. This is important work and we must continue developing and assessing these capabilities today.

Again, I thank you for the opportunity to be here today. I thank all of you, particularly Ranking Member Lugar, for your work keeping the American people safe, and I look forward to any questions you may have.

The CHAIRMAN. Thank you very much, Secretary D'Agostino. I appreciate it.

Let me just mentioned that Senator Udall left, and he asked me—he didn't want to leave, but he is opening the Senate. He is presiding over the Senate. So he had to leave in order to open our session.

Secretary Creedon.

STATEMENT OF HON. MADELYN R. CREEDON, ASSISTANT SECRETARY OF DEFENSE FOR GLOBAL STRATEGIC AFFAIRS, U.S. DEPARTMENT OF DEFENSE, WASHINGTON, DC

Ms. CREEDON. Chairman Kerry, Ranking Member Lugar, and members of the committee, I, too, am pleased to be here today to discuss implementation of the New START Treaty and its implications for our nuclear forces and policy.

But I would like to pause for just a minute and also thank Senator Lugar. As a native Hoosier, it has been with great pride that I have personally enjoyed the leadership of Senator Lugar over the course of the years. And his work in countering the threats of weapons of mass destruction, particularly his work with Senator Nunn in the CTR program, I truly believe is work that has changed the course of history.

And on a personal note, I also want to thank Senator Lugar, who has spoken on my behalf at my confirmation hearing as well. So thank you, sir.

So today I will address not only the implications for our nuclear forces and policy of the New START Treaty, but also some of the misperceptions that have been associated with that treaty and related matters.

Implementation of the New START Treaty is proceeding successfully, and DOD is fully engaged in meeting its treaty obligations. To date, DOD has hosted multiple inspection activities at U.S. strategic facilities and participated in reciprocal activities at Russian strategic facilities.

The Defense Threat Reduction Agency has played a vital role in fulfilling DOD's New START Treaty obligations. Personnel from the Defense Threat Reduction Agency staff, train, equip, and lead the United States teams that conduct onsite inspections in Russia and escort Russian teams inspecting our facilities.

DOD facilities and personnel have been fully prepared to receive Russian inspectors, thanks to the DTRA efforts. The United States is on track to complete the reductions necessary to comply with the New START Treaty's central limits by February of 2018. DOD plans to retain 240 deployed Trident SLBMs on *Ohio* class submarines, up to 60 deployed heavy bombers, and up to 420 single warhead Minutemen III ICBMs.

To meet the treaty's central limits, the administration plans to convert or eliminate a yet-to-be determined combination of ICBM launchers, SLBM launchers, or nuclear-capable heavy bombers. Initial reductions of strategic offensive arms will come from the conversion or elimination of systems accountable under the START Treaty, but no longer maintained in a deployable status; our phantom silos and bombers, which will be focused on first.

Most of the reductions in deployed systems will occur toward the end of the 7-year reduction period. DOD is working to complete a comprehensive drawdown plan, a substantial portion of which will be completed to support the FY 2014 budget request. We are committed to providing Congress with updates on our plans concerning force reductions as they become available.

As the President's budget request for fiscal year 2013 makes clear, DOD is committed to modernizing the delivery systems covered by the New START Treaty that underpin nuclear deterrence. The service life of our current Trident II D5 SLBMs is being extended to 2042. Construction of the first *Ohio* class replacement submarine is now scheduled to begin in 2021.

The administration plans to sustain the Minuteman III ICBMs through 2030, and the United States will maintain two nuclear-capable B–52H strategic bomber wings and one B–2A wing. This year, the Department started a program for a new long-range nuclear-capable penetrating bomber.

DOD is also continuing to develop concepts and technologies associated with boost-glide systems that could provide the basis for a conventional prompt global strike capability. Boost-glide systems would not be subject to the New START Treaty, but I know there is significant interest in those capabilities.

A number of misperceptions have emerged since the New START Treaty was signed. First is that the New START Treaty imposes unilateral constraints on the United States. That is not the case.

New START limits capture both United States and Russian strategic forces and will constrain Russia as it modernizes its delivery systems with several substantially MIRVed new strategic missiles.

Second is that New START included a "secret deal" that places meaningful limits on U.S. missile defenses and conventional prompt global strike capabilities. This, too, is incorrect.

The administration is moving forward to implement all four phases of the European Phased Adaptive Approach for missile defense and will not accept limits on U.S. missile defenses, despite Russia's objections and protests. DOD is funding the continued development and testing of potential conventional prompt global strike capabilities, and while we have no plans to replace nuclear warheads with conventional warheads and ICBMs or SLBMs, the New START Treaty would not prohibit such a decision.

A third critique about the New START is that it fails to capture nonstrategic or "tactical" nuclear weapons within the treaty's limits. The administration is ready to negotiate on nonstrategic as well as nondeployed nuclear weapons with Russia in the next round of arms control talks, as has been made clear when signing the New START Treaty in April 2010 and during the Senate debate over the advice and consent of the ratification of the treaty.

I also would like to reiterate that no one in the administration has walked away from our commitment to modernization, even as the Budget Control Act drives difficult decisions. While the Department has done much to mitigate the efforts of the Budget Control Act, a viable plan to sustain and modernize the nuclear forces, sequestration, however, I should add, would be devastating.

Maintaining strategic stability, assuring allies, and sustaining a safe, secure, and effective deterrent require a partnership between the executive branch and Congress. President Obama has demonstrated his commitment to these priorities, and we hope Congress will demonstrate that same commitment.

Thank you, and I look forward to your questions.

[The prepared statement of Ms. Creedon follows:]

PREPARED STATEMENT OF ASSISTANT SECRETARY MADELYN CREEDON

INTRODUCTION

Chairman Kerry, Ranking Member Lugar, and members of the Committee, I am pleased to appear here today with Acting Under Secretary of State Gottemoeller and Administrator D'Agostino to discuss implementation of the New START Treaty.

I would like to touch on three topics: the status of our implementation of the New START Treaty; its implications for our nuclear forces and policy; and work underway to ensure a future nuclear force structure in line with the President's vision. I would also like to take this opportunity to address some misperceptions associated with the New START Treaty and related matters.

THE NEW START TREATY

As Acting Under Secretary Gottemoeller has discussed in her statement, implementation of the New START Treaty is proceeding successfully. I am pleased to report that DOD is also fully engaged in meeting its obligations under the New START Treaty.

The continuing successful implementation of the New START Treaty is the result of the significant amount of work by many departments and agencies. It is a true interagency partnership and an example of how well our organizations can work together for a common goal—in this case, taking concrete steps toward the President's goal of a world without nuclear weapons.

During the first year of the treaty, the United States and the Russian Federation each completed its annual quota of 18 onsite inspections and both sides appear likely to do so again during Treaty Year Two. The Parties are exchanging updates to their databases on strategic offensive arms twice a year and delegations have met under the Treaty's Bilateral Consultative Commission to discuss implementation issues.

The Department of Defense is responsible for implementing the majority of U.S. obligations under the treaty. Personnel from the Defense Threat Reduction Agency (DTRA) staff, train, equip and lead the U.S. teams that conduct onsite inspections in Russia and escort Russian teams inspecting our facilities. To date, DOD has hosted 29 inspections and exhibitions at U.S. strategic facilities throughout the United States and has participated in 26 inspection activities at Russian strategic facilities. Such onsite inspections are the linchpin of the New START Treaty's verification framework. DTRA inspectors and escorts are responsible for observing, documenting, and reporting the factual findings of their inspection activities to the interagency community responsible for making verification and compliance judgments.

DTRA also works closely with the DOD Office of Treaty Compliance and the military services to maintain the readiness of U.S. facilities for New START inspection activity. This involves working through the inspection procedures for each site, conducting site-assistance visits as needed, and conducting mock inspections. These events provide opportunities for DTRA to simulate actual inspections and refine training for inspection and base personnel. As a result of the DTRA actions, DOD facilities and personnel have been fully prepared to receive the Russian inspectors during the 29 inspections and exhibitions that have taken place in the United States since New START entered into force.

Representatives from DOD serve as essential members of the U.S. delegation to the Bilateral Consultative Commission (BCC)—the bilateral body chartered by the treaty to promote the objectives and implementation of the provisions of the New START Treaty. Since the treaty entered into force in February 2011, the BCC has met three times to discuss and resolve a variety of early implementation issues ranging from the format of inspection activity reports to the amount of telemetric information from strategic ballistic missile launches that the Parties agree to exchange. The Bilateral Consultative Commission builds directly on the experiences and lessons learned from the now-expired START Treaty's Joint Compliance and Inspection Commission (JCIC), and continues the longstanding professional relationship between treaty experts of both Parties. We anticipate the next session of the BCC will be held this fall.

FORCE STRUCTURE

The United States is on track to complete the reductions needed to comply with the New START central limits of 1,550 warheads on deployed intercontinental ballistic missiles (ICBMs), deployed submarine-launched ballistic missiles (SLBMs), and counted for deployed heavy bombers; 700 deployed ICBMs, SLBMs, and heavy bombers; and 800 deployed and nondeployed ICBM and SLBM launchers and heavy bombers by the February 2018 deadline set in the treaty.

The Department of Defense has established a baseline force structure to guide the implementation planning, one that will not require changes to current basing arrangements. The Department plans to retain 240 deployed Trident II D5 SLBMs distributed among *Ohio*-class submarines. This is the most survivable leg of the triad. Recognizing the flexibility of the bomber leg of the triad, we plan to retain up to 60 deployed heavy bombers, including all operational B–2s. Finally, the United States also plans to retain up to 420 deployed single warhead Minuteman III ICBMs.

To achieve this baseline force structure, the United States currently plans to make most of the reductions in deployed systems toward the end of the 7-year reduction period. To meet the treaty's central limits, the administration plans to convert or eliminate a yet-to-be determined combination of ICBM launchers, SLBM launchers, or nuclear-capable heavy bombers.

The initial reductions of the strategic offensive arms will come from the conversion or elimination of systems that were accountable under the START Treaty, but are no longer maintained in a deployable status. These previously retired systems were often referred to as "phantoms" in that they were no longer deployed but still counted under the START Treaty.

These phantoms include 103 empty ICBM launchers and 47 heavy bombers—a total of 150 systems removed from accountability under the New START Treaty. These planned reductions include: 50 empty Peacekeeper ICBM silos at F.E. Warren

U.S. Air Force Base (AFB); 50 empty Minuteman III ICBM silos at Malmstrom AFB; three excess ICBM test silos at Vandenberg AFB; and 34 B–52Gs and 13 B–52Hs currently stored at Davis-Monthan AFB. The estimated cost to eliminate or convert these systems is $47 million.

The Department is working to complete a comprehensive plan for the drawdown, which must be completed no later than February 2018. A substantial portion of this planning effort will be completed to support the FY 2014 budget request. We will continue to maintain the flexibility to make the necessary additional decisions needed to implement these reductions during the latter part of the 7-year drawdown period.

We are committed to providing Congress with updates on our plans concerning these force reductions as they become available.

FORCE MODERNIZATION

As the President's Budget for Fiscal Year 2013 (FY 2013) makes clear, DOD has important work underway to modernize the delivery systems covered by the New START Treaty and that underpin nuclear deterrence. The 2010 Nuclear Posture Review (NPR) concluded that the United States will retain a nuclear triad under the New START Treaty composed of ICBMs, SLBMs, and nuclear-capable heavy bombers; the President's budget request for fiscal year 2013 reflects this commitment.

Sustaining the sea-based leg of our nuclear deterrent is particularly vital as we move to lower numbers under New START. The service life of our current Trident D5 missiles is being extended to 2042. Due to budget constraints, construction of the first *Ohio*-class replacement submarine is scheduled to begin in 2021. While this represents a 2-year slip compared with last year's plan, the Navy believes it can manage the resulting challenges and maintain our commitment to the United Kingdom regarding cooperation in the design of key elements of their new ballistic missile submarines (SSBN). The Navy is planning to build 12 new SSBNs with the first one scheduled to begin patrol in 2031. All DOD sustainment and modernization efforts for the submarine-based strategic nuclear deterrent are fully funded in the President's FY 2013–2017 request.

The administration plans to sustain the Minuteman III ICBM system through 2030, as directed by Congress. Ongoing intensive flight test and surveillance efforts will, by 2017, help determine the investment necessary to achieve that date by providing better estimates for component age-out and system end-of-life. Additionally, the Air Force is nearing completion of a 2-year study examining options and required capabilities for a follow-on ICBM system. The study will make recommendations on whether we should begin a new ICBM development program or initiate a follow-on Minuteman III ICBM life extension program. A small-scale program to maintain a "warm" production line for Minuteman III solid rocket motors was completed this year (FY 2012). A key modernization issue is sustainment of the large-diameter solid rocket motor industrial base. The President's budget request includes $8 million for the Air Force in FY 2013 to study and evaluate a path forward to sustain this key industrial capability.

The United States will maintain two nuclear capable B–52H strategic bomber wings and one B–2A wing. Both bombers, however, are aging and sustainment and modernization funding will have to be provided to ensure they remain operationally effective through the remainder of their service lives. Funding has been allocated to upgrade these platforms; for example, to provide the B–2A with survivable communications, a more modern flight control system, and a new radar. The B–52 will also need various upgrades including for its bomb bay and survivable communications. These modernization and sustainment programs are needed to maintain the effectiveness of the current bomber force until the introduction of a new long-range bomber.

This year, the Department started a program for a new, long-range, nuclear-capable, penetrating bomber that is fully integrated with a family of supporting aircraft and intelligence, surveillance, and reconnaissance assets. Because the growth of modern air defenses is putting even the bomber stand-off missions increasingly at risk, DOD is carrying out an analysis of alternatives (AOA), for a follow-on Air Launched Cruise Missile (ALCM). The final report for the AOA for the new system, the Long-Range Standoff (LRSO) missile, is due in late 2012. The existing ALCM weapon system will be sustained until the LRSO can be fielded during the 2020s.

DOD is also continuing to conduct research and testing to support the development of concepts and technologies associated with boost-glide systems that could provide the basis for a conventional prompt global strike capability. These boost-glide systems are not associated with ICBMs or SLBMs and would not be subject to the provisions of the New START Treaty.

DISPELLING CRITIQUES AND MISPERCEPTIONS

A number of misperceptions have emerged since President Obama and then-Russian President Medvedev signed the New START Treaty in April 2010.

The first misperception is that the New START Treaty imposes unilateral constraints on the United States. This is not the case. The New START Treaty includes a package of negotiated limits that will apply equally to U.S. and Russian strategic forces. Like the United States, Russia will have to limit the number of strategic warheads it deploys to comply with the 1,550 limit of the treaty. This limit will constrain Russia as it modernizes its strategic nuclear delivery systems with the deployments of several substantially MIRVed new strategic missiles, including the MIRVed Yars ICBM, new Borey-class missile submarines carrying 16 MIRVed Bulava SLBMs, and, in the event it is deployed during the life of the treaty, a planned new "heavy" ICBM to replace the SS–18 that will almost certainly carry several MIRVs. Under the New START Treaty, the Russian modernization will be limited to 800 total and 700 deployed strategic delivery systems and 1,550 warheads, the same limits applicable to U.S. systems. And this modernization, given the New START Treaty, does not endanger the ability of U.S. forces to fulfill U.S. deterrence requirements.

The second misperception is that the New START Treaty included a "secret deal" that places meaningful limits on U.S. missile defenses and conventional prompt global strike (CPGS) capabilities. This too is incorrect. The President made clear in his communication to the Congress in December 2010 that the administration will move forward with implementation of all four phases of the European Phased Adaptive Approach to missile defense, and will not accept limits on U.S. missile defenses. We have now deployed an AN/TPY–2 radar in Turkey; secured agreements with Romania and Poland so as to base land-based SM–3 interceptors in each country in the 2015 and 2018 timeframes; and secured an agreement with Spain to host four Aegis BMD-equipped destroyers. Last month at the NATO summit in Chicago, the President announced that as NATO reached an interim ballistic missile defense capability, the United States is now providing support to NATO missile defense by placing the AN/TPY–2 radar under NATO command and control.

We have proceeded down this path despite Russian objections and protests because we agree with our allies that missile defenses are necessary to ensure alliance security in the 21st century. We have also made clear publicly and privately to Russian officials that our missile defenses are being deployed to defend against North Korean and Iranian threats, not to undermine Russia's nuclear deterrent. But to reiterate, we have not limited and will not limit our planned missile defense deployments; indeed, we have made substantial progress since signing the New START Treaty.

As mentioned above, the fiscal year 2013 budget request included funding for the continued development and testing of potential CPGS capabilities. This technology program remains focused on developing and demonstrating boost-glide technologies. When fielded, a CPGS capability could provide the President with a wider range of options to engage targets at strategic ranges in less than an hour, a capability that has previously only been available with nuclear-armed strategic missiles.

While DOD has no plans to replace nuclear warheads with conventional warheads on Minuteman ICBMs or Trident SLBMs, the New START Treaty would not prohibit such a decision. Such systems would, however, remain accountable under the treaty.

In short, there was no "secret deal" constraining U.S. missile defenses or CPGS capabilities.

A third critique about the New START Treaty is that it fails to capture nonstrategic or "tactical" nuclear weapons within the treaty's limits. The United States wants to reduce further the total number of U.S. and Russian nuclear weapons including nonstrategic weapons. The administration made the decision early on not to seek to include nonstrategic and nondeployed nuclear weapons in New START, but to focus on putting in place a successor treaty to the START Treaty set to expire in December 2009, and thus ensure the continuation of verifiable limits on U.S. and Russian strategic nuclear forces. New START strengthens American security by putting new lower limits and a sound verification regime in place. That said, the administration has made clear its readiness to negotiate on strategic, nonstrategic, and nondeployed nuclear weapons with Russia in the next round of arms control talks. This commitment dates back to the President's statement at the signing of the New START Treaty in April 2010 and his communications with the Congress during the debate on advice and consent to ratification of the New START Treaty in 2010. More recently the NATO alliance has signaled its support for this effort in the recently completed Deterrence and Defense Posture Review.

The final misperception associated with New START is that the administration acted in "bad faith" by committing to a modernization program in the "Section 1251 Report" prior to ratification in 2010 and then abandoning the program once the Senate provided its advice and consent to ratification of the treaty. This is also not the case. The administration remains committed to a safe, secure, and effective nuclear arsenal and the nuclear enterprise that supports it and has requested the necessary funding to make that possible. No one in the Obama administration has walked away from our commitment to modernization, even as the Budget Control Act drives difficult decisions. The threat of sequestration, however, does raise significant concerns. While the Department has done much to mitigate the effects of the Budget Control Act to ensure a viable plan to sustain and modernize the nuclear forces, sequestration would be devastating.

CONCLUSION

One of President Obama's first acts as President was to direct a comprehensive approach to address nuclear dangers. The Nuclear Posture Review and the New START Treaty reinforce strategic stability with Russia at lower force levels while ensuring that we have the capabilities necessary for effective deterrence and assurance. DOD continues to strongly support the New START Treaty. Maintaining strategic stability, assuring allies, and sustaining a safe, secure, and effective deterrent require a partnership between the executive branch and the Congress. President Obama has demonstrated his commitment to these priorities; we hope Congress will demonstrate the same commitment.

The CHAIRMAN. Thank you very much.

Senator Lugar, we are going to go to—Bertie, would you? We will go to 7 minutes because of the number of Senators.

Senator LUGAR. Thank you, Mr. Chairman.

Secretary Gottemoeller, I appreciate your recommendations of both the Russian Nuclear Risk Reduction Center and the U.S. Defense Threat Reduction Agency for their efforts during the initial implementation phase.

Could you describe in greater detail the level of professionalism and cooperation between the inspectors of the Russian Nuclear Risk Reduction Center and our own Defense Threat Reduction Agency since the treaty came into force?

Ms. GOTTEMOELLER. Yes, Senator Lugar. I am happy to do so. We actually have a good, I would say, experience base. Some of the inspectors who are now serving as inspectors on the New START Treaty worked on inspections during the START Treaty, and that was 15 years worth of experience accumulated on both the Russian side and the United States side.

They brought that experience to our delegation in Geneva and so helped us to formulate the procedures for the New START Treaty, and I think that has really contributed to the smoothness of implementation so far. The procedures are well understood on both sides, and we have a cadre of professionals who are well schooled in those procedures from their past experience.

And also I would say that their language capability is very good. At our Nuclear Risk Reduction Center, we have a staff working 24/7 with Russian language capability. These notifications, I mentioned 2,500, 2,500 notifications have come in since the beginning of the New START Treaty's implementation, and these are translated immediately when they come across our transom from the Russian Federation.

So it is really a very solid group of professionals on both sides, I would say. And I think that has contributed to a very solid and very positive working environment, as well as getting the job done.

We really truly have been able to, I think, develop a very good understanding of some systems on the Russian side, which we hadn't gotten a good look at before, including primarily the RS–24 new mobile ICBM. We would not have had the depth of knowledge on that system that we have today if it were not for the entry into force of the New START Treaty.

Thank you, sir.

Senator LUGAR. In other words, you have people who, for 15 years, have been doing this job. They have a Russian speaking capability, and they got 2,500 notifications of material. So when they have these spot inspections, they know what they are looking for. They are able to fathom immediately any changes or anything of significance in terms of our defense.

Ms. GOTTEMOELLER. Yes, sir. That is very much the case. It is a combination of inspections and also then declarations they make as they come in to the point of entry, either in Moscow or Ulan-Ude. They notify the Russians about where they want to go for the inspections. So it is a short-notice inspection. The Russians don't know in advance.

And then, when they get to the actual inspection base, that is the point at which we designate a randomly selected missile, for example, for a reentry vehicle onsite inspection. It is only at the moment that we get to the base that the Russians know which missile we are selecting.

So we have a great deal of information from a spectrum of information sources that allow us to then make selections and move through the inspection process. But all of these procedures are very well designated in the inspection protocol of the New START Treaty, and they have proven themselves out in the first year and a half of treaty implementation.

Senator LUGAR. Secretary Creedon, in your opinion, was the executive branch fully prepared to carry out the new requirements negotiated between Moscow and Washington once the New START Treaty was signed and ratified? I have been briefed by DTRA, but tell me what training and exercises were conducted to ensure we were prepared to be fully compliant with the terms of the treaty while protecting our own equities.

Ms. CREEDON. Senator Lugar, as Acting Under Secretary Gottemoeller has said, the DTRA team is well seasoned and well trained and well experienced. They go through rigorous inspections so that they can both host the visiting Russian inspection teams, as well as visit the Russian sites and conduct the inspections at the Russian sites.

They also are closely linked up with the broader nuclear enterprise so that they fully appreciate and understand the U.S. nuclear force structure, nuclear bases, and nuclear systems so that they understand exactly what needs to be protected and what needs to be displayed in the inspection.

So we have very high confidence in them and also appreciate the fact that with the inspectors who had the experience under START, they are able then to also continue training a new generation, if you will, of inspectors.

Senator LUGAR. Secretary Gottemoeller and Secretary Creedon, let me address this question to both of you. You may know that I keep a Nunn-Lugar scorecard in my office that continually reminds me of the impressive level of cooperation between Russian and American officials that has resulted in the elimination of thousands of heavy bombers, ICBMs, ballistic missile submarines.

But as we approach discussions with the Russians on the extension of the Nunn-Lugar umbrella agreement next year, can you both assure me that strategic offensive arms elimination will continue to be a priority for the Obama administration?

Ms. GOTTEMOELLER. I can assure you from the perspective of the Department of State, sir, that this will, in fact, be a strong continuing interest of the United States. I would also—you asked about the process and the diplomacy. We have been preparing the way with the Russians already for the diplomacy that will be required to extend the CTR umbrella agreement.

So that process is already well under way, both at higher levels— I have been in contact with counterparts in the Russian Federation—and also at working level. So it is well in train at this point.

Senator LUGAR. Secretary Creedon.

Ms. CREEDON. Yes, sir. Again, to reiterate what Under Secretary Gottemoeller has said, there have been some good initial discussions and also some good initial responses back from the Russians about the continuation of the umbrella agreement. It is extraordinarily important that we get this resolved fairly early so we don't have any possibility that there might be any sort of a break in the implementation of the CTR program.

Senator LUGAR. I have appreciated monthly reports from the Department of Defense for almost 20 years of how many warheads were taken off that month, how many missiles destroyed, how many silos destroyed. Now that information is in our conference room, available to Russian visitors as well as to Americans. So I appreciate this reassurance.

Thank you, Mr. Chairman.

The CHAIRMAN. Thank you very much, Senator Lugar.

Senator Corker.

Senator CORKER. Mr. Chairman, Senator Isakson was here first, and I know last time had difficulty getting to him. If it is OK with you, I will defer to him first.

The CHAIRMAN. Thank you very much.

Senator Isakson.

Senator ISAKSON. Well, thank you, Senator Corker, and thank you for initiating the letter we both signed to Senator Kerry requesting this hearing today. I appreciate your leadership and appreciate Senator Lugar and Senator Kerry calling this meeting.

I appreciate our witnesses from whom I relied heavily on in my deliberations on the START Treaty 2 years ago. You know, they always criticize us for not reading the bills. I read every blooming page of that thing a couple of times, and Ms. Gottemoeller knows because I had to get her to continue to make definitions for me that I didn't understand otherwise.

So I appreciate very much your input, and I am going to make a statement more than a question, which I would like all three of you to respond to. And I really appreciate the information on the inspections because the heart of this agreement was to trust and verify what the Russian Federation had in terms of nuclear power and if they were complying. And that, of course, is why I think the Russian Federation also wanted the treaty as well.

Now, Senator Corker, myself and others supported this legislation based principally on a final statement from the President with regard to modernization of our nuclear arsenal in the United States of America. I don't want to one day wake up and find out the Russians were doing inspections under the START Treaty in America and found out we were not modernized and competitive anymore.

And I have had some concern on the administration's commitment to modernization. I appreciate Mr. D'Agostino's statement that he thought the President's commitment was evident, but I want to point out a couple of things.

The June 5 letter to Chairman Kerry from Leon Panetta and Steven Chu was a general letter with a lack of specificity on meeting the funding demands. Condition 13, with regard to construction reports and in terms of construction facilities, the President's response in a letter was, and I want to read the phrase correctly, "to the extent possible."

And I made this speech on the floor and never got a response from the administration. So, hopefully, this question will get a response because I would like to see it, Mr. Chairman.

I really need to understand the President's remarks to Dmitry Medvedev a few months ago when he said, thinking the mic was off, "let us get this election behind us and I will be more flexible." I understood that statement to be in reference to missile defense but I don't totally know.

But we cannot afford to be in the business we are in, on this committee or as a country, and be counting on one representation for meeting commitments while, on the other hand, we are seeing a wink and a nod to the other side. So I want you to reaffirm to me your commitment, to the extent possible, to carry out your mission, but understanding that it is important that we receive from the administration a thorough commitment that they are committed to continuing on the paths they set us out on 2 years ago.

Now I understand sequestration is a problem. I understand we have limited resources. We are all dealing with that. But we have made a treaty not just with the Russian Federation, but with the American people and about which is our No. 1 responsibility, which is the safety and the domestic tranquility of the United States. And our nuclear defense is a critical part of that.

So I would like for you too, if you would, address that statement. And I realize it is a statement, and I may be putting you on—and I am not being critical of you. But I want to hear from the administration's highest levels that that commitment is there, and when we do have challenges, we will meet the letter of the law and the letter of the agreements that were made prior to the ratification of the START Treaty.

Mr. D'AGOSTINO. We will start at this end. We will work our way down the table, sir, if that is fine?

Senator ISAKSON. You are the lucky one.

Mr. D'AGOSTINO. I would like to, first of all, say my background. I have been blessed to be able to serve the country in these types of positions for the last 7 years, either in an acting or confirmed status. So I have had an opportunity to observe this and participate actively in this, and I have seen an unprecedented level of commitment on the part of the executive branch toward taking care of our nuclear security enterprise.

It is absolutely unprecedented. We are working on over 80 percent of the stockpile in a very active way, in a way we have never done before, frankly. So the work, the actual work that is going on in taking care of the stockpile is tremendous.

The commitment to themselves and our infrastructure projects, moving forward on the Uranium Processing Facility, the High Explosives Pressing Facility, and a number of other infrastructure projects, is significant and there. You heard the number I mentioned earlier with respect to increases over if the FY13 appropriation and authorization process makes its way through, close to a 20-percent increase in essentially just a little over 2 years, an unprecedented increase as well.

So I have to balance—this isn't, of course, just about dollars. It is about spending the dollars wisely and doing it in a way that we can ensure that the taxpayers are getting what they need and we continue to support the stockpile and get that done.

But even just on the numbers basis alone, it is very significant and demonstrates, in my view, a real commitment. What we have done as a result of the past few years is energize our laboratory workforce in stimulating and developing the people that are actually going to be working on today's stockpile, but will also be there 10 years out into the future to take care of the stockpile and the deterrent so that we can ensure we can maintain it safe, secure, and effective.

We focus a lot on buildings and construction because these are tangible things. But in my experience in this program, and it is close to 20 years in the nuclear weapons program, the key here is making sure that the people get exercised as well. And that is what we have with this budget request.

We are looking forward into the out-years because this is the open question is how are we going to make sure that we can continue these investments in these facilities out in the out-years? And with Madelyn Creedon's team and with the rest of the teams in the Defense Department, we are going to be finishing up the study in the next few months, and we want to make sure that that information gets up to Congress as part of the transparency that was talked about earlier.

I would like to pass it on.

Ms. GOTTEMOELLER. Thank you, Senator Isakson, for your comments, for your remarks, and also I would like to underscore how appreciative I was, but also pressed by your questions. Because you really did want to dive down deep into the details of the inspection regime and the implementation details of the treaty, and I appreciated the opportunity to brief you and at least try to answer your many very serious and important questions.

I thought I would make two remarks. I would like to take up the open mike question that you raised concerning the comments between Medvedev, President Medvedev and President Obama at the Seoul nuclear summit. But I would like to begin by underscoring a clear statement that was made first in the context of the Nuclear Posture Review, but since has been repeated by our President and also by my boss, Senator Hillary—I am sorry, was Senator Hillary Clinton, now Secretary Hillary Clinton.

And that is that the administration absolutely remains committed to a safe, secure, and effective arsenal for as long as nuclear weapons exist. And we do believe that the budget requests that we have been making over these last years have really supported that commitment overall, and we will continue to work very seriously and directly with everyone here on Capitol Hill in order to ensure that those commitments are met.

So I wanted to underscore that commitment for you with its links back to the main policy statement of this administration on nuclear matters, that is, the Nuclear Posture Review.

Second, on the open mike statement, the President was really stating the obvious, I think, sir. He was stating that during this 2012 election year, it is an election year both in the Russian Federation and in the United States of America. It is not going to be a year for breakthroughs.

And so, he was saying that this will be a year where we get the technical experts together. We will have some opportunities to discuss what cooperation may be possible. He and now President Putin got together at Los Cabos in Mexico just this week and discussed this matter and agreed that, first of all, we are committed to looking for ways to cooperate with the Russians on missile defense.

We think that this is in our interests, and it is in the interests of our allies and partners in Europe, as well as the Russian Federation. So we will look for opportunities to cooperate, but we have, I would say, also a very, very clear message—clear and unequivocal—and that is in pursuing this cooperation, we will not in any way allow Russia to have a veto on United States or NATO missile defense plans.

And I think that is very clear. It is a message that the President imparted to his Russian counterpart again this week. So I would just like to say that we look upon 2012 as a work year. We are going to try to do everything we can to develop some pragmatic directions for missile defense cooperation, at the same time bearing in mind that Russia will not have a veto over anything we are doing with our NATO allies or in our own context to develop missile defenses.

Thank you.

The CHAIRMAN. Senator Shaheen.

Senator SHAHEEN. Thank you, Mr. Chairman.

The CHAIRMAN. What? Oh, did you—I don't want to cut you off an answer, but I think it has been answered is my sense.

Senator ISAKSON. I am satisfied with the answer. Thank you, Mr. Chairman.

The CHAIRMAN. Thank you very much, Senator. Appreciate it.

Senator Shaheen.

Senator SHAHEEN. Well, thank you, Mr. Chairman.

And I am sorry that I missed the testimony from all of our panelists. I know that there has been—I just heard a little bit of Senator Isakson's questions about whether or not we are actually funding modernization in the way that we should, and I do think it is important to point out, as I am sure you already have, that there was a requested 5-percent increase. And in this fiscal environment, while it is not what I think some people would have liked, it is, I think, a difficult decision in the fiscal environment that we are in to provide additional funding.

But the real question I think is whether we have the funding that we need to maintain the health of the nuclear stockpile, and I wonder if you could just answer whether you think, in your opinion, the budget that was presented will allow us to do that—to maintain the health of the stockpile. And I don't know if one of you wants to answer that or if all three of you would like to?

Mr. D'AGOSTINO. Senator Shaheen, I will start the answer. The answer is "Yes," we absolutely do have the resources we need if the FY13 request is authorized and appropriated as requested.

It is very important, you did note the 5-percent increase in the weapons activities account. What isn't really always talked about, frankly, is within that weapons activities account, the part that actually supports the stockpile is actually going up by $420 million, or 7.2 percent.

So that is a very significant increase, and it is an increase for good reason because it is working aggressively on about 80 percent—life extension work on 80 percent of the stockpile. So, yes, I am quite comfortable with the request.

Maybe one of my colleagues might care to add?

Ms. CREEDON. Thank you, Senator.

I just want to add on behalf of the Defense Department and the work of the Nuclear Weapons Council, which is the joint DOE, NNSA, Department of Defense group that makes sure and oversees the entire nuclear enterprise, and on that score, the Department of Defense and Department of Energy are working very closely to make sure that the ongoing modernization work and life extension work of the NNSA continues to meet the requirements of the Department.

And we are, in fact, meeting the requirements under the auspices of the Weapons Council.

Senator SHAHEEN. Good. Thank you.

I know that we have heard a lot about how New START has benefited us, but I wonder if we could examine a little bit the implications of where we would be if we had not passed New START.

So, first, in March 2011, the Russian Federation conducted an exhibition for United States officials of the new RS–24 ICBM mobile missile, first time Americans had a chance to see that up close and personal. And I wonder if we think this exhibition would have been possible without New START in place?

Ms. Gottemoeller.

Ms. GOTTEMOELLER. No, sir. No, ma'am. I'm sorry. It would not have been possible without the New START Treaty.

Senator SHAHEEN. And would we have the insight that we do into Russia's strategic forces without New START, and why is that important to have that information and those insights?

Ms. GOTTEMOELLER. First of all, we do have our own national technical means, intelligence means. We are constantly monitoring the Russian strategic forces. This is a very important aspect of our national security.

Of course, it helps us to understand what exactly our Strategic Command needs to plan for in terms of ensuring that our national security is really guaranteed through our own nuclear deterrence forces and their operational planning and targeting capabilities. So it is very important from the perspective of our national security to understand everything we can.

So we do have some tools available to us, but it is through the mechanism of onsite inspection of strategic arms reduction treaties that we are actually able to get our inspectors in on the ground and have an opportunity to really look, as you put it, up close and personal at the Russian strategic nuclear weapons systems, whether it is their submarine launch systems, their ICBMs, both mobile and fixed ICBMs, or their bomber forces.

So it is really the best way that we can get eyes on and really have that kind of confidence in what is going on. And that is the whole point of the treaty and has been the point of this effort since we started strategic arms limitation back in the 1970s. The point is to have enhanced predictability and enhanced knowledge and transparency between the two sides so that we do not get into the kinds of crises that dogged us during the worst days of the cold war.

Particularly, the signal example is the Cuban missile crisis. And that shock to our two capitals, Washington and Moscow, I think led us down the road of looking for ways to enhance predictability and mutual confidence between—we are the two biggest nuclear countries in the world. So to enhance confidence and have that kind of stability and transparency is really to the benefit of our national security and international security as well.

Senator SHAHEEN. Thank you.

Ms. Creedon, the former commander of STRATCOM, General Chilton, testified during the treaty consideration that "without New START, we would rapidly lose insight into Russia's nuclear force and would be left to use worst-case analyses."

I assume that without the insight and without the stability and certainty of the treaty, you would agree with General Chilton that the Department of Defense would have a much more difficult and costly time planning our strategic weapons programs and policies?

Ms. CREEDON. Yes, ma'am. That is absolutely true. And in these times of constrained budget environments, I think it is even more true and more important.

Senator SHAHEEN. Thank you.

And Mr. D'Agostino, I believe you have testified in a similar fashion that New START has allowed you to better plan and use your agency resources more effectively. So is it safe to say that that stability and confidence that is provided by New START really allows you to better plan for modernization of our nuclear complex?

Mr. D'AGOSTINO. Yes, ma'am. It absolutely does that because these investments are investments over long periods of time. Having that stability allows us to be efficient in our planning process and execution.

Thank you.

Senator SHAHEEN. Thank you.

And Ms. Creedon, as I mentioned, the entire military establishment unanimously supported the ratification of New START. Is it safe to say that today's leadership continues to strongly support the treaty?

Ms. CREEDON. Yes, ma'am. Absolutely, all the way from the Secretary to the Chairman to the Vice Chairman to all the senior leadership of the Department and all the senior military leaders.

Senator SHAHEEN. And I assume they would be opposed to curtailing the implementation of the treaty?

Ms. CREEDON. Absolutely.

Senator SHAHEEN. Thank you.

Ms. Gottemoeller, one of the real positive aspects of the treaty, it seems to me, has been the bipartisan support that it has enjoyed really from the first passage of the START Treaty back in as early as 1992, when that was originally passed. As we went back and looked up the votes for each of the treaties before this hearing, and they were 93 to 6, 87 to 4, and 96 for the START II and 95 to 0 for the SORT Treaty in 2003.

Can you just talk about why you think that is important as we move forward on implementation of this New START Treaty?

Ms. GOTTEMOELLER. Yes, ma'am. It has been the case that there has been a strong consensus across our political spectrum really since the days when President Nixon first began these negotiations. I mentioned strategic arms limitation back in the early 1970s.

President Reagan, of course, was the very strong impetus behind negotiation of both the Intermediate Range Nuclear Forces Treaty and the START Treaty in the 1980s. And so, I think I can say that it has been an executive branch matter of really working on both sides of the aisle because, again, of the importance to national security of having the predictability and mutual confidence of these kinds of treaties.

They are hard slogging, as we all know, and I do appreciate the way Senators on both sides of the aisle during the difficult START ratification debate were really concerned and interested to have their questions answered thoroughly. And we were very glad to see that seriousness of purpose and to engage because I think this is a very serious matter.

But traditionally, it has been a matter that has enjoyed the strong support of both Presidents and Senators on both sides of the aisle.

Senator SHAHEEN. Thank you.

I am sorry, Mr. Chairman, for using more than my time was allotted.

The CHAIRMAN. Appreciate it. Thank you.

Senator Corker.

Senator CORKER. Thank you, Mr. Chairman. Thanks for having the hearing. I appreciate it very much and appreciate you following up on that.

And certainly, Ranking Member Lugar's comments on the front end, I appreciate those very much. And again, to second what others have said, years and years of leadership on this kind of issue, and I think all of us thank you for that and hope, as was mentioned, that that will continue.

But thank you very much.

To the witnesses, I enjoyed very much working with Secretary Gottemoeller during the process. I didn't really spend much time with you, Ms. Creedon, but thank you for being here today.

And I know that my questions are really outside both of your areas, more to D'Agostino. For what it is worth, I have been highly disappointed in the followthrough on modernization. Highly disappointed.

And it disappoints me, actually, Administrator D'Agostino, to hear you talk about the unprecedented increase when you know that you are still not living up to the commitments that have been made. And I know that in many ways, you are a foot soldier in this and other people are making decisions, and you are having to put on a good face. Maybe you like putting on a good face. I don't know.

But I am very disappointed in the followthrough.

The fact is the administration has not lived up to what was agreed to. I don't know how in the world you could know what you are saying to Senator Shaheen when the 1251 isn't even out yet that is due in July.

So I have to tell you I am losing faith in your ability to carry out what was agreed to in this. And I know that, again, other people are involved in many of the decisions that are taking place.

And actually, what I see happening, I see the President out now announcing further reductions. It seems like things are being slow-walked. And I almost wonder as the President is announcing further reductions, the reason that much of the modernization is being slow-walked is that there is no intention to follow through, and they actually hope to come up with more reduction so that much of the modernization that we are talking about does not have to take place.

And I will let you answer that first big question, and then I want to get into some others. But I don't know how anybody could be happy with the followthrough on modernization as has been put in place. It has been like the Keystone Kops, for what it is worth, in Congress.

There has been no support from the administration whatsoever in trying to cause these appropriations to be coordinated and seen through. None whatsoever. It is almost everybody is pointing fingers in multiple directions, and that has been highly frustrating.

And I think Senator Lugar said it best. It is going to take leadership from the administration to make this happen.

It has not been there, and yet I would like for you to respond to my first question, and I will ask you more.

Mr. D'AGOSTINO. Certainly, Senator. Thank you very much.

I can assure you there is no slow-walking going on. It certainly might appear that way, and I don't want to—certainly can't speak for your perspective——

Senator CORKER. Well, from my standpoint, can you understand why it would appear that way?

Mr. D'AGOSTINO. Yes, sir. Absolutely. I understand your point.

Senator CORKER. OK. But we have not honored the deal that was laid out. Is that correct?

Mr. D'AGOSTINO. There is a very significant investment in the infrastructure——

Senator CORKER. Well, have we honored what was laid out in the 12——

Mr. D'AGOSTINO. Yes, absolutely. The President asked for in his fiscal year 2011 budget request very significant investments. We were fortunate to receive an anomaly by Congress in order to do that. We were still $223 million short in that anomaly. Despite that case, we received with the President requested full funding for these projects in the fiscal year 2012 budget——

Senator CORKER. He did not request it this year, though.

Mr. D'AGOSTINO [continuing]. $300 million.

Senator CORKER. Did he request it this year?

Mr. D'AGOSTINO. He did not receive funding from Congress in order to do these projects.

Senator CORKER. Last year. What about this year?

Mr. D'AGOSTINO. This year, our goal is to maintain the plutonium capabilities. The key in my view is the right investments to maintain capabilities, and that is exactly what the President has asked for in his FY13 budget.

Senator CORKER. Let me ask you this. If the President wants to reduce the nuclear capabilities of our country, which apparently he has just announced he wants to do, it seems to me that he would intentionally slow-walk these because he is hoping that our nuclear arsenal will be much less than it is today.

I mean, would that not be a rational place for him to be?

Mr. D'AGOSTINO. Absolutely not. We need these facilities, and the President has not canceled the facilities. We need these facilities and, more importantly, the capabilities these facilities present no matter what, no matter whether the arsenal was one warhead or no matter whether the arsenal is the current 1,550 operationally deployed warheads that we currently have right now under New START.

So these facilities are absolutely required. The President understands that. That is why this particular budget in FY12 fully requested funds, which we didn't get, in order to do that. That is why our fiscal year 2013 budget fully requests the funds to work on over 80 percent of the stockpile, make investments in high explosive pressing, make investments in Uranium Processing Facility, make investments in maintaining our plutonium capabilities.

Senator CORKER. Let us talk about plutonium. Before we entered into this agreement, the reuse of plutonium pits was not acceptable. Now, all of a sudden, it is acceptable.

I just find that to be fascinating, and there is no plan whatsoever. I think we have laid out the need for 50 new plutonium pits each year. You have no plan in place whatsoever to make that happen, and yet you say that this is moving along as it is supposed to move along.

We talked a little bit about this yesterday, but I am just fascinated by this change. And right after the treaty is signed, this change in thoughts as it relates to Los Alamos and plutonium pits.

Mr. D'AGOSTINO. Senator Corker, I am not familiar with the phrase saying that reuse of plutonium pits is not acceptable. I have never said that, and I have been in the program for a while.

Senator CORKER. Do we have plans to cause them to be used in a proper way? Can you tell me today how we are going to do that?

Mr. D'AGOSTINO. I can tell you in a closed session specifics on how we were planning on reusing pits, and I can tell you specifically in a closed session on the numbers specifically as it relates to taking care of the stockpile.

The Nation has a very significant number of plutonium pits. We have done extensive lifetime studies over the last 20 years on plutonium. We have a high degree of confidence in the quality of the materials that have been made in the past, and we should take advantage of what the Nation has invested in over the last longer—frankly, longer than 20 years in making pits.

But that still doesn't mean we don't need to maintain a plutonium capability. And in fact, the FY 2013 budget proposes to do exactly that. We do need it both authorized and appropriated in order to move forward.

Senator CORKER. Secretary Creedon, you know, we gave you the ability to transfer $125 million to NNSA. That has not happened. Can you tell me why that hasn't happened?

Ms. CREEDON. Senator, as Mr. D'Agostino has said, the FY13 budget for NNSA, based on FY12 funding levels, is adequate for the work in 2013. That said, the Nuclear Weapons Council continues to review all the programs of the NNSA and the modernization programs at DOD.

And I would note that right now there are——

Senator CORKER. That was 2012 authority I am talking about, and I am talking about FY12 authority to transfer. I don't think you all did that.

Ms. CREEDON. Right. No, that is what I am saying.

Senator CORKER. OK.

Ms. CREEDON. The 2012 authority, based on what we are looking at from the 2012 program and then looking into the 2013 program, at the moment, they appear to be on track based on the funding that they have received. But we are continuing to look at the overall program.

I think you are aware that we have instituted a joint DOD/NNSA study to look at how to rebuild this program into the future. And the other thing I should point out is that the Weapons Council has now approved additional work on life extension program. So right now, the NNSA has ongoing life extension work, and looking at studying life extension work on three different systems and possibly four, which is more than they have ever worked on historically in terms of life extension programs.

But if and when we do see a need, then we recognize that we have this authority. But at the moment, we haven't identified that need yet. That is not to say we won't when the ongoing study is completed.

Senator CORKER. Mr. Chairman, again, I thank you for the time, and I know I am—probably my temperature is a little higher today than normal. But I will just say that this U.S. Senator feels very let down by the administration on modernization.

And while you talk about increases, and we have had increases. I agree with that, and that was obviously very important to me. They have not met what was laid out during the modernization agreements and the ratification, candidly, that was laid out when the treaty was passed.

And for what it is worth, this one U.S. Senator would be very reticent to agree to any treaty with this administration on any topic until something changes as it relates to the commitments on this START Treaty. And I know you all are talking in a positive way about this.

This has been the most frustrating process I have been involved in in the U.S. Senate is again trying to get the various entities coordinated in such a way as we moved ahead, as was planned. We had no help whatsoever, none, during the appropriations process from the administration.

And I want to thank the Senator for having this hearing. I thank him for the way he candidly handled the process itself. I enjoyed very much working with him, but I could not be more disappointed in the administration in the followthrough.

And this has been a learning experience for me. I just want everybody to know that, and I hope that everybody will get their act together, move ahead, before any other treaties, especially of this nature, ever come before the United States Senate on this topic.

Thank you very much.

The CHAIRMAN. Thank you, Senator Corker.

The vote-a-thon has started, and so we are going to wrap up in a moment. But I want to address what Senator Corker has said, and I also want to ask a couple of questions before we wrap up. And I would like Senator Corker to be here to be part of this. I want to see if we can get this on track here.

I want to associate myself with the remarks of Senator Isakson and—to some degree, I don't agree with Senator Corker that— I think when the House of Representatives cuts the budget, it is not the fault of the administration. But I think we have to figure out why Senator Corker feels that there is not an adequate pressure here on the funding component of this because I want to say, in association with the comments of Senator Isakson, we worked hard together to build a consensus to pass the treaty.

And our word is as involved in this as your word, and I think it is critical that we follow through. Now, obviously, we can't have a weapon structure that is not sufficiently modernized that people make a judgment that the deterrent is there and working. But, I mean, there is a complicated overall picture here because the general trend line, if you look at General Cartwright's comments recently and others, is a belief that we can have an adequate deterrent and make the world safer and save a significant amount of money with still further reductions in the amount of nuclear weapons that are out there actively.

I believe that. I think we are still stuck at a much higher number than is necessary in today's world.

Not everybody, obviously, is convinced of that, and we have some people who don't like any reductions. So this is a fight that is going to go on for some period of time. It is critical to build confidence at every level in order to be able to approach this fight correctly.

So can you sort of address, I mean, I want you to speak to this sense that Senator Corker has that somehow the funding wasn't what it was supposed to be. Secretary D'Agostino, do you want to speak to that?

Mr. D'AGOSTINO. Absolutely. I think when we plan our programs, we look not just at 1 year because, as was mentioned earlier, these are multiyear programs. Investments to build a multibillion dollar facility require typically 8 to 12 years worth of commitment, which is important to have.

We also take advantage of new things that happen as a result, and things have changed in the last year. Not relating to the specifics associated externally, as was discussed, but mostly in my program, we realized that the existing investments in the new Chemistry and Metallurgy Research building, the radiation building, allowed us to do a lot more plutonium work in there than we had previously expected.

This is a result of new analysis, technical analysis. So instead of operating with about 6 to 8 grams of plutonium in this facility, we can now go up to close to 40 grams of plutonium. That increases the workload that the laboratory Los Alamos and Livermore can do in an existing brand-new facility, which we just opened up this week, which is a result of support from Congress and the previous administrations and this administration.

So we have learned in the last year not just that we have had challenges fiscally, which, of course, we recognize that. And of course, we learned that we didn't get the FY12 appropriation like we asked, but we've learned also that we can do a lot more work in the existing facilities. And that takes the risk away from the plutonium capability question that this is a go/no-go decision.

The CHAIRMAN. Well, let me sort of cut to the quick of it because we are not going to have time. Unfortunately, we are in the second part of the vote.

But one of the things the Navy did for me before I went off to Vietnam was to send me to chemical/nuclear/biological warfare school, and I learned a fair amount about all of this. And I followed it, I think, pretty diligently since I came to the Senate in 1985, and we debated the MX missile and Europe and tactical nuclear and a whole bunch of things here.

But when you measure concepts of deterrence and choices in terms of war and peace and weapons you might use and not use, one has to stop and think pretty clearly about whether you think you would declare war on China or going into a nuclear exchange with China, who have a mere fraction of the weapons that we have. And most rational people would decide they don't want 1 or 2 or 3 of them fired, let alone 10 or 20, let alone 100.

So apart from the ideology and sort of some of the things that have driven this race for, you know, the entire last half of the last century and the first 12 years of this one, we need to think carefully about what is the appropriate level. And I think this is going to be forced on us in the context of our budgets over these next years anyway.

But I ask you this big question in a sense. In the first year-plus of the treaty's operation, is the Russian Federation acting in, or has it acted in, a manner that is inconsistent with the object and purpose of the treaty? Just yes or no, very quick.

Ms. GOTTEMOELLER. No, sir. They have been acting in the spirit of the treaty.

The CHAIRMAN. And is there any way that they have acted that would threaten the national security interests of the United States?

Ms. GOTTEMOELLER. No, sir. In the context of this treaty, I think they have been implementing their obligations, and certainly, it is, in my view and the view of others in the administration, enhancing the national security of the United States.

The CHAIRMAN. And all of you, each of you, has Russia attempted to move beyond the treaty's limits in any militarily significant way or any way that we can measure?

Ms. GOTTEMOELLER. No.

The CHAIRMAN. Secretary D'Agostino.

Mr. D'AGOSTINO. No, sir.

The CHAIRMAN. Secretary Creedon.

Ms. CREEDON. No, sir.

The CHAIRMAN. And with the current level of expenditure that we are putting into modernization, can you say with certainty to the United States Senate and the country that our weapons are fully functional, protected, and on a track to remain so in the foreseeable future?

Mr. D'AGOSTINO. Yes, sir. Absolutely. Our weapons and our stockpile are safe, secure, and effective, and they are reliable. Very confident of that.

The CHAIRMAN. Secretary Gottemoeller.

Ms. GOTTEMOELLER. Yes, sir. And I would underscore once again that the President has said as we pursue further reductions in nuclear weapons, we must sustain a stockpile that is safe, secure, and effective.

So Mr. D'Agostino's earlier comment that whether we have hundreds, thousands, or one, we will still have to have a very capable, responsive nuclear weapons infrastructure. I think that is absolutely the case.

The CHAIRMAN. So you are confident that we are deploying—and as we come into 2018 and the treaty requires us to have no more than 1,550 deployed warheads—are you confident that we would be deploying a stockpile that is then safe, secure, and reliable?

Mr. D'AGOSTINO. Yes, sir. With support from Congress and authorization/appropriation, this administration will continue to provide that out in the future, and I trust future administrations will as well.

The CHAIRMAN. Secretary Gottemoeller.

Ms. GOTTEMOELLER. Yes, sir. I agree with Mr. D'Agostino's comment. Working closely in partnership with the Congress to ensure the appropriations and authorizations help us to achieve that goal.

The CHAIRMAN. Secretary Creedon.

Ms. CREEDON. Yes, sir. And I also want to add that although we haven't talked about it much today, the delivery systems that are the responsibility of the Department of Defense are also undergoing significant modernization programs. And that this is very much a team effort between DOD and the NNSA when we shape and formulate these programs going forward to ensure that we have a safe, secure, and effective deterrent into the future.

The CHAIRMAN. Now I understand the House of Representatives may want to block the military from deploying the warhead number set forth in New START unless NNSA gets every dime of the resources planned November 2010.

I would assume that it doesn't really help your concerns if Congress winds up forcing you into a situation where you have more deployed warheads than you had anticipated, and you still don't get the resources you need.

That is not going to help, is it?

Mr. D'AGOSTINO. It would make it very challenging, and it would cause us to further have to probably cut different things to keep focus just on the stockpile, but then longer term investments would be led astray.

The CHAIRMAN. Well, I want to thank you all for being here today. Thank you for the work you are doing. I think it is vital to our country. I think you have been doing an exemplary job. I think you negotiated a tough treaty under difficult circumstances.

And as we go forward here, we need to just stay in touch, work together, and I am confident we can get the job done.

Thank you all very much for being here today. We stand adjourned.

[Whereupon, at 11:25 a.m., the hearing was adjourned.]

ADDITIONAL MATERIAL SUBMITTED FOR THE RECORD

RESPONSES OF ACTING UNDER SECRETARY ROSE GOTTEMOELLER TO QUESTIONS SUBMITTED BY SENATOR RICHARD G. LUGAR

STATUS OF THREAT REDUCTION AGREEMENTS WITH RUSSIA

Within calendar year 2013, there appears to be a possibility that, for the first time in decades, the United States will not have in place the set of agreements that have governed and implemented U.S. threat reduction in that nation. Former President Medvedev signed a decree on August 11, 2010, announcing Russia's intention to withdraw from the 1992 International Science and Technology Center (ISTC) Agreement. Even while preparations are underway for a transition of the ISTC from Russia to another former Soviet Republic, the Nunn-Lugar Umbrella Agreement and the U.S.-Russia HEU Purchase Agreement also expire in 2013.

Question. Has President Putin, or any other Russian official, yet provided a formal, written notification to the ISTC of a decision to withdraw from the ISTC pursuant to Article XV of the agreement establishing the ISTC?

Answer. On August 11, 2010, Russian President Medvedev issued a decree announcing adoption of the Government of the Russian Federation's proposal to withdraw from the 1992 Agreement Establishing the International Science and Technology Center (Agreement). The International Science and Technology Center (ISTC) is headquartered in Moscow. The decree directed The State Corporation for Atomic Energy "Rosatom," together with other interested federal agencies, to carry

35

out work relating to withdrawal of the Russian Federation from the Agreement and 1993 Protocol on the Provisional Application of the Agreement (Protocol).

The decree also directed the Ministry of Foreign Affairs with the participation of Rosatom to notify each Party to the Agreement and the Protocol through diplomatic channels of the decision, and stated that the Agreement and Protocol would be null and void for the Russian Federation 6 months after the date of such submission of such written notification to the other parties. (The Agreement and Protocol specify that a party may withdraw 6 months after notice to the other parties.) Such a written notification has not yet been provided.

On July 13, 2011, the Ministry of Foreign Affairs of the Russian Federation sent diplomatic notes to the United States and the other parties to the Agreement informing them of its intention to terminate the provisional application of the Agreement and to withdraw from the Protocol, and to take these actions in accordance with the provisions of the Agreement and the Protocol upon completion of the last of the Russian projects that are currently being implemented with the financial participation of the ISTC by the middle of 2015.

UPLOAD UNDER LOWER NUMBERS

Former Chairman of the Joint Chiefs of Staff Admiral Mullen stated in answers to my questions in 2010 that:

> New START . . . provides the United States with the flexibility to deploy, maintain, and modernize its strategic nuclear forces in the manner that best protects U.S. national security interests. The U.S. will retain the ability to "upload" a significant number of nuclear warheads as a hedge against any future technical problems with U.S. delivery platforms or warheads, a technical breakthrough by an adversary that threatens to neutralize a U.S. strategic delivery system, or as a result of a fundamental deterioration in the international security environment.

A recent press article I submit for the record states that an "[administration] official floated the possibility of reducing the number to about 1,000" and that "The United States would also explore the possibility for unilaterally abandoning a portion of [its] roughly 3,000 reserve warheads."

(STORY FOLLOWS)

U.S. TO UNVEIL NEW PLANS TO FURTHER REDUCE NUCLEAR ARSENAL—WASHINGTON, JUNE 16, KYODO NEWS

(HTTP://ENGLISH.KYODONEWS.JP/NEWS/2012/06/164247.HTML)

U.S. President Barack Obama is slated to compile and unveil soon, possibly by the end of this month, plans to further reduce the country's nuclear arsenal, high-level U.S. officials said Friday.

The U.S. government would seek, through future negotiations with Russia, a substantially larger reduction in operational strategic nuclear weapons from the 1,550 the United States is allowed to maintain under a new START treaty with Moscow.

The United States would also explore the possibility for unilaterally abandoning a portion of the roughly 3,000 reserve warheads not yet deployed, the officials said.

While the Obama administration is making final adjustments over the size of the reduction target for operational strategic nuclear weapons, one official floated the possibility of reducing the number to about 1,000. Nuclear experts close to the Obama administration have put the figure at between 1,000 and 1,100. The administration's plans to seek additional cuts in nuclear weapons reflects Obama's aspiration to seek a world without nuclear weapons as proclaimed in a speech in Prague, the Czech Republic, in April 2009.

But the administration plans to make no unilateral cuts in strategic nuclear weapons, instead seeking reassurances from Moscow through a new treaty or a political agreement that Russia would make similar reductions, the officials said. Russia, for its part, is warily watching its Cold War adversary over concern that U.S. efforts to build an antiballistic shield in Europe could render Russia's strategic nuclear weapons ineffective, showing no sign that it would be willing to respond to a U.S. offer. Obama's new operational guidelines for nuclear weapons would be the culmination of work launched after his administration concluded the so-called Nuclear Posture Review in 2010.

The Obama administration has argued that one of the principal roles nuclear weapons play in U.S. policy is to provide a so-called "nuclear umbrella" to such U.S. allies as Japan and South Korea. The administration concluded in its latest review that the United States can maintain an effective nuclear deterrent even if it maintains fewer than the 1,550 strategic nuclear weapons stipulated under the New Strategic Arms Reduction Treaty with Russia, according to the officials. The option of reducing them to the 300 level was discussed but eventually dismissed as insufficient to maintain a credible deterrent, the officials said. The United States currently has about 5,000 nuclear weapons in its stockpile, of which just below 2,000 are operational strategic nuclear weapons, 200 are shorter-range operational tactical weapons, and about 3,000 reserve nuclear warheads. Separately, it has about 3,000 warheads waiting to be dismantled.

Question. Do either of you believe that the ability of the United States to execute effective responses to serious noncompliance with Article II of the New START Treaty through uploading its reserve warheads would be imperiled by cuts as outlined in the press?

Answer. The administration intends to pursue further reductions (below New START levels) in concert with Russia, and would like these reductions to include strategic, nonstrategic, and nondeployed nuclear weapons.

As stated in the 2010 Nuclear Posture Review (NPR), the U.S. goals in post-New START bilateral negotiations with Russia will include reducing nonstrategic nuclear weapons together with the nondeployed nuclear weapons of both sides. The NPR also makes clear that U.S. nuclear force reductions will maintain the reliability and effectiveness of security assurances to our allies and partners.

EFFECTIVE VERIFICATION—TIMELY RESPONSES TO SIGNIFICANT VIOLATIONS

The standard of effective verification was established during consideration of the INF Treaty. Testifying before the Foreign Relations Committee on the INF Treaty in 1988, Ambassador Paul Nitze provided the definition of "effective verification." He stated: "What do we mean by effective verification? We mean that we want to be sure that, if the other side moves beyond the limits of the treaty in any militarily significant way, we would be able to detect such a violation in time to respond effectively and thereby deny the other side the benefit of the violation."

With regard to the New START Treaty, the committee heard testimony in closed session from U.S. intelligence community witnesses and from New START negotiators. The committee also reviewed both public and classified materials on these issues, including: (a) the National Intelligence Estimate (NIE) on U.S. capabilities to monitor Russian compliance with the treaty; (b) the State Department's report on the verifiability of the treaty, provided pursuant to section 306(a)(1) of the Arms Control and Disarmament Act (22 U.S.C. 2577(a)(1)); and, (c) a letter from the Secretary of Defense that summarized the Defense Department's assessment of the military significance of potential Russian cheating or breakout, based on the 2010 New START NIE on monitoring the treaty.

Question. With regard to each of the documents and testimony cited above, please stipulate whether a U.S. unilateral decision to go well below New START Treaty aggregate Article II numbers would affect any key judgments contained in any of the relevant documents and testimony provided to the Senate in 2010 regarding U.S. upload responses to noncompliance.

Answer. The administration intends to pursue further reductions (below New START levels) in concert with Russia, and would like these reductions to include strategic, nonstrategic, and nondeployed nuclear weapons.

The verification regime for New START is a detailed and extensive set of data exchanges and timely notifications covering all strategic offensive arms and facilities covered by the treaty, as well as onsite inspections, exhibitions, restrictions on where specified items may be located, and additional transparency measures. These verification mechanisms enable us to monitor and inspect Russia's strategic nuclear forces to ensure compliance with the provisions of the treaty.

FUTURE AGREEMENTS WITH RUSSIA—NEGOTIATING LEVERAGE

In 2010, Secretary Clinton said "Leverage for future negotiations will come from several directions. The Russians are concerned with the totality of the U.S. nuclear stockpile, particularly the upload capability of our strategic ballistic missiles."

Question. Why would the United States consider unilateral cuts or constraints on future delivery systems outside of any negotiations if such systems provide leverage in future negotiations with Moscow, per the Secretary's statement regarding American upload capability?

Answer. The administration intends to pursue further reductions (below New START levels) in concert with Russia, and would like these reductions to include strategic, nonstrategic, and nondeployed nuclear weapons.

UNILATERAL CUTS

The Resolution of Ratification for the New START Treaty that I authored and which was agreed to in this Committee and the Senate included a declaration stating: "The Senate declares that further arms reduction agreements obligating the United States to reduce or limit the Armed Forces or armaments of the United States in any militarily significant manner may be made only pursuant to the treaty-making power of the President as set forth in Article II, section 2, clause 2 of the Constitution of the United States."

Question. Is this administration considering any unilateral reductions in any categories of U.S. nuclear weapons outside of any treaty with Russia, or otherwise?

Answer. The administration intends to pursue further reductions (below New START levels) in concert with Russia, and would like these reductions to include strategic, nonstrategic, and nondeployed nuclear weapons.

Question. If so, how would such reductions be consistent with existing statute (22 U.S.C. 2753(b)) and the Senate's declaration on New START?

Answer. The administration is not considering any arms reductions that would be outside the scope of 22 U.S.C. 2753(b) or the Senate's declaration on New START.

GOING LOWER

Question. The New START Treaty allowed each side 7 years to reach its treaty compliant force structure, and to modify it over the life of the treaty. Freedom to mix and match systems, and to modernize, are guaranteed by the treaty. To date, the administration has not yet been clear with regard to how it would structure our forces during the next 6 years, prior to the time when the United States must be "at or below" Article II limits.

If it was the administration's intention to "go lower," then why did it not simply extend the START I Treaty, and negotiate a treaty covering deployed, nondeployed and nonstrategic systems as the follow-on to START I?

Answer. In March 2006, the Russian Federation advised the United States that it was not inclined to extend the START Treaty in its current form. In October 2006, the United States concurred that the START Treaty should not be extended, though some provisions of that treaty might be carried forward.

Thus, a simple extension of the START Treaty was not a viable option, and the administration adopted the goal of concluding a new treaty to replace the START Treaty.

ENRICHMENT AND REPROCESSING IN 123 AGREEMENTS

Earlier this year, the administration adopted a "case-by-case" policy with respect to application of a standard such as may be found in the Agreed Minute to the 2009 123 Agreement with the United Arab Emirates regarding enrichment and reprocessing (ENR). Administration policy is to submit 123 agreements with new countries that do not contain ENR commitments, such as the agreement with Vietnam or Jordan.

Question. Is it true that under the revised Guidelines regarding ENR transfers adopted by the Nuclear Suppliers Group (NSG) that neither Jordan nor Vietnam would qualify for transfers of enrichment technology?

Answer. Under the existing Nuclear Suppliers Group Guidelines, we consider it highly unlikely that any supplier would transfer enrichment technology to either Jordan or Vietnam regardless of whether they meet the criteria. Neither country in the foreseeable future is expected to develop a nuclear power program of sufficient magnitude to justify the establishment of a domestic uranium enrichment capability. Additionally, Vietnam does not have an Additional Protocol in force, and Jordan is not a Party to the Convention on the Safety of Spent Fuel Management and the Safety of Radioactive Waste Management. Having an Additional Protocol and adherence to relevant nuclear safety conventions (not further defined) are two of the relevant criteria to qualify for transfers.

Question. If so, then why is the administration apparently no longer seeking ENR commitments from Jordan or Vietnam?

Answer. The administration is currently conducting 123 agreement negotiations with both Jordan and Vietnam. While we are not able to comment publicly on the details of those ongoing negotiations, we are discussing assurances on ENR with both countries.

Question. Will either the Jordan or Vietnam 123 agreements be submitted to Congress this year?

Answer. While it is still a possibility, I do not think it likely that the President will submit any proposed 123 agreements to the Congress in 2012.

Question. You are currently serving as Acting Under Secretary of State for Arms Control and International Security, but you have not been nominated to that position by the President. The Vacancies Reform Act establishes limits on the amount of time an official may serve on an acting basis in a position requiring the advice and consent of the Senate. You have also been permitted to continue serving in the Assistant Secretary position to which you were confirmed in 2009.

- On what date did you begin serving as Acting Under Secretary of State for Arms Control and International Security (U/S T)?

Answer. I began serving as the Acting Under Secretary for Arms Control and International Security (T) on February 7, 2012.

Question. What is the Department of State's understanding as to how much longer you may continue to serve as an Acting Under Secretary of State if you are not nominated to that position by the President?

Answer. According to the Vacancies Reform Act, if the President has not submitted a nomination, an acting officer may serve in an acting capacity for 210 days from the date of the vacancy.

Question. You have stated that "I want to stress that I am continuing with my responsibilities as U.S. Assistant Secretary for Arms Control, Verification, and Compliance [A/S AVC]. But now I'll combine my previous functions with the responsibilities of Under Secretary for Arms Control and International Security." You have also stated "In the simplest terms, AVC is the Arms Control Bureau." As both an Under Secretary and an Assistant Secretary with negotiating and other arms control functions, are you and the Department of State under the understanding that you remain the full-time Assistant Secretary that fully participates in all interagency groups or organizations within the executive branch of the U.S. Government that assesses, analyzes, and/or reviews United States planned or ongoing policies, programs, or actions that have a direct bearing on verification, or compliance and enforcement matters, including interagency intelligence committees concerned with the development or exploitation of measurement or signals intelligence or other national technical means of verification, as Congress intended in Subtitle A of Title XI of Public Law 106–113?

Answer. Yes.

Question. When Congress created the Assistant Secretary slot in which you now serve, and the Verification Bureau, the State Department originally countered by offering to create a position within the office of U/S T for verification. Please explain how combining your duties as both U/S T and A/S AVC will not result in verification issues being treated in the manner the Department originally proposed, and Congress rejected, in Public Law 106–113?

Answer. It is the view of the Department of State that, according to the Vacancies Reform Act, I am required to continue in my position as Assistant Secretary for Arms Control, Verification and Compliance (AVC). This Bureau, created by Public Law 106–113 and with responsibilities as spelled out in the State Department Foreign Affairs Manual, continues to have responsibility for overall supervision of arms control, verification, and compliance issues within the Department of State. The 144 employees of the AVC Bureau are constantly working to ensure that the vital arms control, verification, and compliance mission is carried out in support of U.S. national security. This includes offices and individuals solely dedicated to developing verification approaches and technology, monitoring compliance, developing verification and compliance assessments, and a 24/7 watch to monitor compliance. The President's designation of me as Acting Under Secretary was not intended to, and did not, transfer the AVC Bureau's statutory functions of verification and compliance to the Office of the Under Secretary.

RESPONSES OF ASSISTANT SECRETARY MADELYN R. CREEDON TO QUESTIONS
SUBMITTED BY SENATOR RICHARD G. LUGAR

NUNN-LUGAR UMBRELLA AGREEMENT/SOAE

Nunn-Lugar executes program activities in Russia under both the U.S.-Russia
CTR Umbrella Agreement and the Agreement Between the Department of Defense
of the United States of America and the Russian Federal Space Agency Concerning
Cooperation in the Elimination of Strategic Offensive Arms (the SOAE Implementing Agreement).

Question. On July 2, 2008, the Russian Duma ratified the 2006 Extension Protocol
and the 1999 Extension Protocol to the CTR Umbrella Agreement. On what date
in 2013 do either of these agreements expire?

Answer. The current CTR Umbrella Agreement expires on June 17, 2013. However the U.S. Government is seeking to extend it for 7 years beyond that date.
Unless it is terminated by either party, the SOAE Implementing Agreement, as
extended in 2006, remains in effect for the duration of the Umbrella Agreement, as
amended or extended.

Question. Should the U.S.-Russia CTR Umbrella Agreement expire, or lapse with
no successor agreement in place, or Russian ratification of a protocol to extend it
not occur before expiration, could the Department of Defense continue to undertake
activities in Russia under the SOAE Implementing Agreement?

Answer. The SOAE Implementing Agreement will expire upon expiration of the
CTR Umbrella Agreement. To continue undertaking activities, the United States
would need an extension, or some other successor agreement, in place.

Question. In the last decade, when the protocol to extend the U.S.-Russia CTR
Umbrella Agreement was not submitted to the Duma before the expiration of the
existing text (though it was eventually ratified), how were Department of Defense
personnel and U.S. contractors able to continue to undertake destruction of strategic
weapons delivery systems and associated infrastructure in Russia?

Answer. The Nunn-Lugar program began operating in the Russian Federation
under an Umbrella Agreement entitled "The Agreement Concerning the Safe and
Secure Transportation, Storage and Destruction of Weapons and the Prevention of
Weapons Proliferation" (CTR Umbrella Agreement) signed on June 17, 1992. The
CTR Umbrella Agreement entered into force upon signature. In 1999, a Protocol was
concluded that extended and amended the CTR Umbrella Agreement. The 1999 Protocol was provisionally applied from the date of its signature until its entry into
force in 2008. In 2006 an additional Protocol that further extended the CTR
Umbrella Agreement was concluded. The 2006 Protocol was also provisionally
applied from the date of signature until such time as it entered into force, which
occurred at the same time in 2008 as entry into force of the 1999 Protocol.

SOAE ACTIVITIES IN RUSSIA

The FY 2013–FY 2017 Implementation Plan for SOAE in Russia calls for: (a) continued elimination of SS–25 road-mobile launchers and SS–25 ICBMs; (b) infrastructure elimination at SS–25 Strategic Rocket Forces bases; (c) SS–N–20 SLBM
elimination efforts (to have been completed in FY 2012); (d) dismantlement and
elimination of SS–18 and SS–19 ICBM silos and ICBMs; (e) dismantlement and
elimination of SS–N–18 SLBMs; and (f) elimination and dismantlement of SLBM
launchers, the Delta III- and Typhoon-class Russian SSBNs.

Question. Please provide, in classified form if necessary, and with regard to (a)-
(f), above, a summary of the launchers, ICBMs, SLBMs, and associated infrastructure that Russia has indicated will be slated for elimination or dismantlement in
fiscal years 2013 and 2014 under the Nunn-Lugar program.

Answer. Russia does not formally indicate in advance which missiles will be
slated for elimination. However, Russia's Federal Space Agency (FSA) recently estimated that, in 2013, it plans to request CTR assistance in the elimination of nine
SS–25 ICBMs and road-mobile launchers, and four SS–N–18 SLBMs. FSA representatives stated that these plans were estimates for the first half of 2013 but
withheld plans for the full calendar year until they better understood whether the
CTR Umbrella Agreement will be extended beyond its current expiration of June
2013. Russia's State Atomic Energy Corporation "Rosatom" has also requested CTR
support for the dismantlement of Delta III, Hull 393 in 2013, and DOD has agreed
to support this project. Russia has offered no estimate for 2014.

Question. Please provide, in coordination with the intelligence community, a statement as to the utility for treaty monitoring purposes of the continuation of SOAE activities in Russia.

Answer. Information exchanges and verification measures required under the New START Treaty (NST), including notifications and inspections, provide sufficient transparency to enable the United States to verify eliminations of Russian strategic systems. Information from SOAE activities often plays a confirmatory role in evaluating NST data and sometimes provides limited advance notice of Russian elimination activity.

Question. Is there any circumstance under which the Department of Defense would no longer seek to carry out SOAE activities in Russia?

Answer. DOD constantly assesses the ongoing threat reduction value of CTR projects. If the threat reduction value of SOAE in Russia is no longer evident, DOD will likely phase out SOAE work.

Question. If so, why?

Answer. DOD constantly assesses the ongoing threat reduction value of CTR projects. If the threat reduction value of SOAE in Russia is no longer evident, DOD will likely phase out SOAE work.

Question. The administration stated in an answer for the record in 2010 that in determining whether any newly developed elimination procedures under New START are sufficient, the United States will not limit itself to a predetermined set of criteria. Please provide a description of how U.S. dismantlement of a Russian system governed under paragraph (8) of Article III of the New START Treaty, and relevant portions of the New START Protocol and Annexes, is done so as to ensure that no elimination procedures used by the United States in Russia could result in ambiguous situations affecting the viability and effectiveness of the New START Treaty.

Answer. CTR's SOAE program takes the conversion or elimination requirements of the New START Treaty and uses them as a baseline from which to add any additional elimination processes deemed mutually beneficial.

STATUS OF THREAT REDUCTION AGREEMENTS WITH RUSSIA

Within calendar year 2013, there appears to be a possibility that, for the first time in decades, the United States will not have in place the set of agreements that have governed and implemented U.S. threat reduction in that nation. Former President Medvedev signed a decree on August 11, 2010, announcing Russia's intention to withdraw from the 1992 International Science and Technology Center (ISTC) Agreement. Even while preparations are underway for a transition of the ISTC from Russia to another former Soviet Republic, the Nunn-Lugar Umbrella Agreement and the U.S.-Russia HEU Purchase Agreement also expire in 2013.

Question. Has President Putin, or any other Russian official, yet provided a formal, written notification to the ISTC of a decision to withdraw from the ISTC pursuant to Article XV of the agreement establishing the ISTC?

Answer. On August 11, 2010, then-President Medvedev issued a decree announcing adoption of the Government of the Russian Federation's proposal to withdraw from the 1992 Agreement Establishing the International Science and Technology Center (ISTC Agreement). The International Science and Technology Center (ISTC) is headquartered in Moscow. The decree directed the State Corporation for Atomic Energy "Rosatom," and other state agencies to carry out work relating to the withdrawal of the Russian Federation from the ISTC Agreement and 1993 Protocol on the Provisional Application of the ISTC Agreement (Protocol).

The decree also directed the Ministry of Foreign Affairs, with the participation of Rosatom, to notify each Party to the ISTC Agreement and the Protocol through diplomatic channels of the decision, and stated that the ISTC Agreement and Protocol would be null and void for the Russian Federation 6 months after the date of such submission of such written notification to the other Parties. (The ISTC Agreement and Protocol specify that a party may withdraw 6 months after notice to the other parties.) Such a written notification has not yet been provided.

On July 13, 2011, the Ministry of Foreign Affairs of the Russian Federation sent diplomatic notes to the United States and the other Parties to the ISTC Agreement informing them of its intention to terminate the provisional application of the ISTC Agreement and to withdraw from the Protocol, and to take these actions in accordance with the provisions of the ISTC Agreement and the Protocol upon completion of the last of the Russian projects that are currently being implemented with the financial participation of the ISTC by the middle of 2015.

Question. The Department of Defense is an ISTC partner and manages Biological Threat Reduction Program (BTRP) projects in Russia through the ISTC because there is no BTRP implementing agreement with Russia. If the ISTC is no longer to be located in Russia, how would the Department of Defense conduct any BTRP activities in Russia in the future?

Answer. DOD expects to complete ongoing work by the time of Russia's planned withdrawal date of 2015. However, DOD is exploring other options for continuing BTRP cooperation with Russia.

Question. Please provide a summary as to the legal status, relationships among, the expiration date, necessity for future activities under and negotiating status (if relevant, to include whether a new text has been provided to the Russian Government) of each of the following:

- (a). The Agreement Between the United States of America and the Russian Federation Concerning the Safe and Secure Transportation, Storage and Destruction of Weapons and the Prevention of Weapons Proliferation, dated June 17, 1992, as amended February 3, 2005, and as amended and extended June 15/16, 1999 and June 16, 2006 (the U.S.-Russia CTR Umbrella Agreement);

Answer. The U.S.-Russia CTR Umbrella Agreement provides overarching terms that enable the cooperative activities that the U.S. Government undertakes with the Government of Russia to safely secure and destroy weapons of mass destruction and related materials and establish additional verifiable measures against proliferation of such weapons. The current CTR Umbrella Agreement expires on June 17, 2013. However the U.S. Government is seeking to extend it for 7 years beyond that date.

- (b). The Agreement Between the Department of Defense of the United States of America and the Federal Agency for Industry Concerning the Safe, Secure and Ecologically Sound Destruction of Chemical Weapons, dated July 30, 1992, as amended March 18, 1994; May 28, 1996; April 10, 1997; December 29, 1997; January 14, 1999; November 14, 2000; August 29, 2002; October 23, 2002; March 17, 2003; March 18, 2003; September 23, 2003; July 28, 2004; October 6, 2005; September 8, 2006; and May 21, 2007 (Chemical Weapons Destruction Implementing Agreement);

Answer. Unless it is terminated by either Party, the Chemical Weapons Destruction Implementing Agreement remains in force for the duration of the Umbrella Agreement, as amended or extended.

- (c). The Agreement Establishing an International Science and Technology Center, dated November 27, 1992 (ISTC Agreement);

Answer. The ISTC Agreement remains in effect, although Russia has indicated it will withdraw by mid-2015. Prior to President Medvedev's August 11, 2010, decree announcing Russia's intention to withdraw from the ISTC Agreement, the United States made a major effort to interest Russia in continuing multilateral non-proliferation and other scientific cooperation—either in a "transformed" ISTC or in a "new framework" of broadened scientific scope. In the course of discussions with the relevant agencies of the Russian Government, it was made clear that Russia felt it no longer needed assistance in providing employment for its scientists and that there was not sufficient support for continuing such cooperation. President Medvedev's decree announcing Russia's intention to withdraw has made it almost inevitable that the ISTC headquarters in Moscow will close and Russia will leave the organization.

In the wake of the Medvedev decree, the administration has been working with the other funding Parties and the ISTC's non-Russian former Soviet Union (FSU) member states to preserve the ISTC by moving the headquarters elsewhere. The June 27, 2012, Governing Board (GB) meeting gave approval in principle to moving the ISTC to Kazakhstan and negotiation is beginning for necessary amendments to the existing ISTC Agreement to reflect Russia's withdrawal, as well as other amendments that might serve to make the organization a more flexible instrument for the future. The Department of State is preparing to enter such negotiations with the remaining ISTC Parties.

Preserving the ISTC will both provide a multilateral means to continue addressing our ongoing concerns in the region and keep open the possibility that Russia might decide to associate itself again with the ISTC at some future point.

- (d). The Agreement Between the Department of Defense of the United States of America and the Federal Space Agency Concerning Cooperation in the Elimination of Strategic Offensive Arms, dated, August 26, 1993, as amended April 3, 1995; June 19, 1995; May 27, 1996; April 11, 1997; February 11, 1998; June 9, 1998; August 16, 1999; August 8, 2000; June 9, 2003; September 25, 2003; January 14, 2005; May 25, 2006; and April 27, 2007; and as amended and extended August 30, 2002 and September 5, 2006 (SOAE Implementing Agreement);

Answer. Unless it is terminated by either party, the SOAE Implementing Agreement remains in force for the duration of the Umbrella Agreement as amended or extended.

- (e). The Memorandum of Understanding and Cooperation on Defense and Military Relations Between the Department of Defense of the United States of America and the Ministry of Defense of the Russian Federation, dated September 8, 1993 (Defense and Military Contacts MOU);

Answer. In 2006, a Protocol (2006 Protocol) that further extended the CTR Umbrella Agreement was concluded. The 2006 Protocol included an annex listing the agreements to which the provisions of the CTR Umbrella Agreement apply. This annex excluded the Defense and Military Contacts MOU.

- (f). The Agreement Between the Government of the United States of America and the Government of the Russian Federation on Science and Technology Cooperation, dated December 16, 1993 (Science and Technology Cooperation Russia Implementing Agreement);

Answer. The U.S.-Russia Science and Technology Agreement (Agreement) was extended on December 16, 2005, for a 10-year term; the Agreement would expire by its terms on December 15, 2015. At the next meeting of the Science and Technology Working Group under the Bilateral Presidential Commission, currently scheduled for March 2013, the United States will propose to merge the Science and Technology Working Group and the Joint Science and Technology Committee Meeting called for under the Agreement. The DOD CTR Program currently conducts its science and technology cooperation with Russia through the ISTC Agreement and the ISTC Funding Memorandum of Agreement.

- (g). The Agreement Between the Department of Defense of the United States of America and the Ministry of Defense of the Russian Federation Concerning Cooperation in Nuclear Weapons Storage Security through Provision of Material, Services, and Related Training, dated April 3, 1995, as amended June 21, 1995; May 27, 1996; April 8, 1997; January 14, 1999; November 1, 1999; June 12, 2000; September 19, 2002; July 12, 2004; May 5, 2005; March 22, 2006; February 21, 2007; and November 15, 2007 and as extended January 14, 1999; January 25, 2000; and June 17, 2006 (NWSS Implementing Agreement);

Answer. Unless it is extended, the NWSS Implementing Agreement will expire by its terms on June 17, 2013. However, the U.S. Government will seek to extend it for 7 years beyond that date along with the Umbrella Agreement.

- (h). The Agreement Between the Department of Defense of the United States of America and the Ministry of Defense of the Russian Federation Concerning Cooperation in Nuclear Weapons Transportation Security through Provision of Material, Services, and Related Training, dated April 3, 1995, as amended June 21, 1995; May 27, 1996; June 12, 2000; February 28, 2002; September 19, 2002; March 26, 2003; March 5, 2004; July 12, 2004; May 23, 2005; August 26, 2005; March 22, 2006; and February 21, 2007; and as extended January 14, 1999; January 25, 2000; and June 17, 2006 (NWTS Implementing Agreement);

Answer. Unless it is extended, the NWTS Implementing Agreement will expire by its terms on June 17, 2013. However, the U.S. Government will seek to extend it for 7 years beyond that date along with the Umbrella Agreement.

- (i). The Memorandum of Agreement Between the Government of the United States of America and the International Science and Technology Center Concerning the Contribution of Funds for Approved Projects to Facilitate the Nonproliferation of Weapons and Weapons Expertise, dated April 15, 1996, as amended by annexes May 23, 1997; May 21, 1998; and January 26, 1999; and by amendments to the annex of January 26, 1999; June 29, 1999; and September 18, 2000 (ISTC Funding Memorandum of Agreement).

Answer. The ISTC Funding Memorandum of Agreement remains in force and, unless a Party withdraws from it, it will remain in force for the duration of the ISTC Agreement.

LIABILITY ISSUES WITH RUSSIA

The original Nunn-Lugar program operated in the Russian Federation from 1992 to 1999 under an umbrella agreement that was negotiated in 1991 and 1992. That agreement was submitted to the Russian Duma and was approved and therefore carried the force of law. The Nunn-Lugar program functioned quite well under that for 7 years. In 1999, the umbrella agreement expired of its own terms and was signed again by the Governments of the United States and the Russian Federation. The Russian Federation did not submit the umbrella agreement to the Duma for timely ratification even after it was successfully renegotiated (though that did eventually happen). It was applied on a de facto basis in the intervening period, with Russian and American cooperation.

Question. What liability protections for threat reduction activities exist in Russia outside of our existing agreements with Russia (as listed in question 12)?

Answer. In addition to the liability protections for threat reduction activities provided by our existing bilateral agreements with Russia, there may be some protection applicable to activities in Russia and certain surrounding countries against liability for nuclear damage arising from certain threat reduction activities through the Vienna Convention on Civil Liability for Nuclear Damage (Vienna Convention) to which Russia is a Party. (The Vienna Convention would not provide protection against lawsuits in U.S. courts because the United States is not a Party to the Vienna Convention.) Under the Vienna Convention, liability for nuclear damage arising from a nuclear incident at a nuclear installation in Russia would be channeled to the operator of the installation. We do not know whether Russia would argue that the Vienna Convention does not cover certain nonpeaceful uses and that threat reduction activities are a nonpeaceful use not covered by the Vienna Convention.

Question. Does the Russian Government fear that liability might be imposed on it in the case of an incident of liability involving Nunn-Lugar activities and, if so, why have they not developed an adequate doctrine to protect Russian interests but instead tried to shift liability to the United States?

Answer. In the past, Russia has not expressed concern regarding its responsibility for damage arising out of Russian actions in connection with Nunn-Lugar activities. Rather, the issue has been whether Russia should assume responsibility for damages, if any, allegedly caused by the U.S. Government, its employees, or its contractors in carrying out Nunn-Lugar activities.

The Nunn-Lugar program began operating in the Russian Federation under an Umbrella Agreement entitled "The Agreement Concerning the Safe and Secure Transportation, Storage and Destruction of Weapons and the Prevention of Weapons Proliferation" (CTR Umbrella Agreement) signed on June 17, 1992. The CTR Umbrella Agreement entered into force upon signature. In 1999, a Protocol was concluded that extended and amended the CTR Umbrella Agreement. The 1999 Protocol was provisionally applied from the date of its signature until its entry into force in 2008. In 2006 an additional Protocol that further extended the CTR Umbrella Agreement was concluded. The 2006 Protocol was also provisionally applied from the date of signature until such time as it entered into force, which occurred at the same time in 2008 as entry into force of the 1999 Protocol.

NPR IMPLEMENTATION STUDY

Both press reports and conversations with various administration officials have revealed that the administration decided to delay completion the Nuclear Posture Review (NPR) Implementation Study and that it could result in changes to Presidential guidance affecting employment of the force, and perhaps significant cuts in U.S. nuclear forces well below Article II of the New START Treaty.

Question. What is the status of the Defense Department's implementation study for the 2010 NPR?

Answer. The NPR Implementation study continues. As the review has not been formally completed, I cannot comment on specific content. However, once the study has been completed, the intent is to brief Congress following authorization by the President.

Question. The administration has refused to share Presidential Policy Directive 11 (PPD 11) with the Congress, but has stated that the numbers of warheads, missiles, and launchers in the New START Treaty reflect extant guidance from the previous administration. Is the Department of Defense prepared to share with this committee either the PDD from this administration or the guidance from the Bush administration well before the time when another treaty with Russia might be presented to the Senate?

Answer. During the New START Treaty ratification hearings, a briefing was provided to the SFRC and SASC on November 17, 2010. This briefing, titled "New START Treaty Force Exchange Analysis," provided an overview of Presidential guidance as well as USSTRATCOM force planning. It is our intention to brief you well before presentation of any potential new treaty to the Senate.

UPLOAD UNDER LOWER NUMBERS

Question. Former Chairman of the Joint Chiefs of Staff, Admiral Mullen, stated in answers to my questions in 2010 that: "New START . . . provides the United States with the flexibility to deploy, maintain, and modernize its strategic nuclear forces in the manner that best protects U.S. national security interests. The U.S. will retain the ability to 'upload' a significant number of nuclear warheads as a hedge against any future technical problems with U.S. delivery platforms or warheads, a technical breakthrough by an adversary that threatens to neutralize a U.S. strategic delivery system, or as a result of a fundamental deterioration in the international security environment."

A recent press article I submit for the record states that an "[administration] official floated the possibility of reducing the number to about 1,000" and that "The United States would also explore the possibility for unilaterally abandoning a portion of [its] roughly 3,000 reserve warheads."

(STORY FOLLOWS)

U.S. TO UNVEIL NEW PLANS TO FURTHER REDUCE NUCLEAR ARSENAL—WASHINGTON, JUNE 16, KYODO NEWS

(HTTP://ENGLISH.KYODONEWS.JP/NEWS/2012/06/164247.HTML)

U.S. President Barack Obama is slated to compile and unveil soon, possibly by the end of this month, plans to further reduce the country's nuclear arsenal, high-level U.S. officials said Friday.

The U.S. Government would seek, through future negotiations with Russia, a substantially larger reduction in operational strategic nuclear weapons from the 1,550 the United States is allowed to maintain under a new START treaty with Moscow.

The United States would also explore the possibility for unilaterally abandoning a portion of the roughly 3,000 reserve warheads not yet deployed, the officials said.

While the Obama administration is making final adjustments over the size of the reduction target for operational strategic nuclear weapons, one official floated the possibility of reducing the number to about 1,000. Nuclear experts close to the Obama administration have put the figure at between 1,000 and 1,100. The administration's plans to seek additional cuts in nuclear weapons reflects Obama's aspiration to seek a world without nuclear weapons as proclaimed in a speech in Prague, the Czech Republic, in April 2009.

But the administration plans to make no unilateral cuts in strategic nuclear weapons, instead seeking reassurances from Moscow through a new treaty or a political agreement that Russia would make similar reductions, the officials said. Russia, for its part, is warily watching its cold war adversary over concern that U.S. efforts to build an antiballistic shield in Europe could render Russia's strategic nuclear weapons ineffective, showing no sign that it would be willing to respond to a U.S. offer. Obama's new operational guidelines for nuclear weapons would be the culmination of work launched after his administration concluded the so-called Nuclear Posture Review in 2010.

The Obama administration has argued that one of the principal roles nuclear weapons play in U.S. policy is to provide a so-called "nuclear umbrella" to such U.S. allies as Japan and South Korea. The administration concluded in its latest review that the United States can maintain an effective nuclear deterrent even if it maintains fewer than the 1,550 strategic nuclear weapons stipulated under the New Strategic Arms Reduction Treaty with Russia, according to the officials. The option of reducing them to the 300 level was discussed but eventually dismissed as insufficient to maintain a credible deterrent, the officials said. The United States currently has about 5,000 nuclear weapons in its stockpile, of which just below 2,000 are operational strategic nuclear weapons, 200 are shorter-range operational tactical weapons, and about 3,000 reserve nuclear warheads. Separately, it has about 3,000 warheads waiting to be dismantled.

- Do either of you believe that the ability of the United States to execute effective responses to serious noncompliance with Article II of the New START Treaty through uploading its reserve warheads would be imperiled by cuts as outlined in the press?

Answer. Our nondeployed hedge requirements under the New START Treaty are being analyzed as part of the ongoing Nuclear Posture Review Implementation Study. As the review has not been formally completed, I cannot comment on specific content. Once complete, we intend to brief Congress on the results of the study. At that time, we will be able to address this question.

Question. Former Secretary Gates also stated in 2010 that "[U.S.] upload capability will be more than sufficient under New START."

- (a). If it was more than sufficient under New START, could you furnish the analysis to this committee that this administration has done regarding what sufficient upload capability would be available to the United States if it were to eliminate warheads from its nondeployed hedge and/or make cuts that would eliminate a leg of our Triad?

Answer. To date, no final decisions have been made with respect to force structure under the New START Treaty; such decisions will be informed by the ongoing Nuclear Posture Review (NPR) Implementation Study. These decisions will be consistent with the goals of the 2010 NPR, including to: maintain strategic deterrence and stability at reduced nuclear force levels; strengthen regional deterrence and provide assurance to our allies and partners; maintain a nuclear triad; and maintain a safe, secure, and effective nuclear deterrent.

- (b). Would this administration, now or at any time in the future, entertain the notion of U.S.-Russian parity in upload capability in a future treaty?

Answer. As the 2010 Nuclear Posture Review stated, large disparities in nuclear capabilities could raise concerns on both sides and among U.S. allies and partners, and may not be conducive to maintaining a stable, long-term strategic relationship, especially as nuclear forces are significantly reduced. The large imbalance in Russia's nonstrategic nuclear stockpile relative to that of the United States is a clear reason why we need an arms control arrangement that lowers overall numbers. The administration would entertain the notion of U.S.-Russian parity in overall warhead numbers—recognizing both the imbalance in Russia's nonstrategic nuclear stockpile and our advantage in upload capability—in a future treaty.

EFFECTIVE VERIFICATION TIMELY RESPONSES TO SIGNIFICANT

The standard of effective verification was established during consideration of the INF Treaty. Testifying before the Foreign Relations Committee on the INF Treaty in 1988, Ambassador Paul Nitze provided the definition of "effective verification." He stated: "What do we mean by effective verification? We mean that we want to be sure that, if the other side moves beyond the limits of the Treaty in any militarily significant way, we would be able to detect such a violation in time to respond effectively and thereby deny the other side the benefit of the violation."

With regard to the New START Treaty, the committee heard testimony in closed session from U.S. intelligence community witnesses and from New START negotiators. The committee also reviewed both public and classified materials on these issues, including: (a) the National Intelligence Estimate (NIE) on U.S. capabilities to monitor Russian compliance with the treaty; (b) the State Department's report on the verifiability of the treaty, provided pursuant to section 306(a)(1) of the Arms Control and Disarmament Act (22 U.S.C. 2577(a)(1)); and, (c) a letter from the Secretary of Defense that summarized the Defense Department's assessment of the military significance of potential Russian cheating or breakout, based on the 2010 New START NIE on monitoring the treaty.

Question. With regard to each of the documents and testimony cited above, please stipulate whether a U.S. unilateral decision to go well below New START Treaty aggregate Article II numbers would affect any key judgments contained in any of the relevant documents and testimony provided to the Senate in 2010 regarding U.S. upload responses to noncompliance.

Answer. As stated in the Nuclear Posture Review, the United States is committed to a long-term goal of a world free of nuclear weapons. Further, any future reductions must continue to strengthen deterrence of potential regional adversaries, strategic stability vis-a-vis Russia and China, and assurance of our allies and partners.

The United States will continue to ensure that, in the calculations of any potential opponent, the perceived gains of attacking the United States or its allies and partners would be far outweighed by the unacceptable cost of the U.S. response. As did my predecessor, I assess that Russia would not be able to achieve militarily significant cheating or breakout under the New START Treaty, due to both the New START Treaty verification regime and the inherent survivability and flexibility of the planned U.S. strategic force structure. Speculation on potential impacts of any future U.S. reductions of any sort absent details on the proposed scale and timing of the hypothesized unilateral reductions is not possible.

Question. Please provide an analysis of American ability to respond to militarily significant violations of the New START Treaty should the United States decide to (a) eliminate ICBMs or heavy bomber-accountable weapons and/or (b) unilaterally to reduce or eliminate any warhead that does not count toward the aggregate limit specified in clause (b) of paragraph (1) of Article II of the New START Treaty as applied to deployed ICBMs, deployed SLBMs, and deployed heavy bombers.

Answer. DOD is continuing to study the final force structure and will announce end-state force structure decisions at a later date. In general, however, the U.S. force structure changes under the New START Treaty will ensure that the United States maintains the ability to hedge effectively against technical and geopolitical developments by preserving our capability to upload, as well as to change our force posture as necessary. As stated in the 2010 Nuclear Posture Review Report, the United States also is committed to achieving these objectives by maintaining all three legs of the nuclear Triad under the New START Treaty—ICBMs, heavy bombers, and SSBNs.

With respect to reductions or eliminations of warheads, the United States maintains nondeployed nuclear warheads in the U.S. stockpile to provide logistics spares, support the Quality Assurance and Reliability Testing program, and hedge against technical or geopolitical developments. The nondeployed stockpile currently includes more warheads than would be required for these purposes. Progress in restoring NNSA's production infrastructure will also allow the United States to reduce its reliance on, and thus further reduce the supply of, reserve warheads. Again however, any such reductions will be designed to account for possible adjustments in the Russian strategic force configuration.

CONDITION (9) REPORT

Question. Condition (9) of the December 22, 2010, Senate Resolution of Advice and Consent to the Ratification of the New START Treaty required that if appropriations are enacted that fail to meet the resource requirements set forth in the President's 10-year plan, or if at any time more resources are required than estimated in the President's 10-year plan, the President shall submit to Congress, within 60 days of such enactment or the identification of the requirement for such additional resources, as appropriate, a report detailing (1) how the President proposes to remedy the resource shortfall; (2) if additional resources are required; (3) the impact of the resource shortfall on the safety, reliability, and performance of United States nuclear forces; and (4) whether and why, in the changed circumstances brought about by the resource shortfall, it remains in the national interest of the United States to remain a Party to the New START Treaty. We did not receive this report until June of this year, well after 60 days since the enactment of lower levels of appropriations for nuclear weapons in fiscal year 2012.

• Why did it take so long to submit this report?

Answer. We apologize for the delay in submitting the report. The primary reason the report is late is because of the analysis and assessment required by Condition 9 of the Senate's Resolution of Advice and Consent to the Ratification of the New Start Treaty. This analysis took time to complete and formed the basis of information provided in DOD's Report prepared in response to section 1043 of the National Defense Authorization Act for Fiscal Year 2012 that was submitted to Congress in May 2012. The logical sequencing of reports placed initial priority on completing the Section 1043 Report before the Condition 9 report. The Condition 9 report was completed and submitted to Congress approximately 1 month after the Section 1043 Report.

UNCERTAINTY

Former Secretary Gates stated in 2010 that "The limits and verification provisions of the New START Treaty, if it is ratified and enters into force, will reduce uncertainty relative to what it otherwise would have been the case, and therefore will reduce the requirement for the United States to hedge."

Question. How many of the warheads within the nondeployed hedge are necessary to maintain a credible and effective hedge both (a) at Article II limits of the New START Treaty and (b) below them?

Answer. The Department of Defense continues to assess that Russia will not be able to achieve militarily significant cheating or breakout under the New START Treaty without our detecting such a violation in time to respond effectively. This assessment is based on both the Treaty's verification regime and the inherent survivability and flexibility of the planned U.S. strategic force structure. The United States retains a hedge against technical and geopolitical developments, including Russian noncompliance.

Question. If the administration does take a decision to reduce or eliminate some number of American nondeployed warheads, do the New START Treaty's annual quota of 10 Type One inspections, data exchanges, notifications, unique identifiers, and our extant National Technical Means provide you with sufficient confidence to state that if Russia were ever to be in noncompliance with Article II's central limit of 1,550 warheads on deployed ICBMs, deployed SLBMs, and nuclear warheads counted for deployed heavy bombers, that United States could effectively and in a timely manner respond to Russian noncompliance?

Answer. The Department of Defense continues to assess that Russia will not be able to achieve militarily significant cheating or breakout under the New START Treaty without our detecting such a violation in time to respond effectively. This assessment is based on both the Treaty's verification regime and the inherent survivability and flexibility of the planned U.S. strategic force structure. The United States retains a hedge against technical and geopolitical developments, including Russian noncompliance.

GOING LOWER

The New START Treaty allowed each side 7 years to reach its treaty-compliant force structure, and to modify it over the life of the treaty. Freedom to mix and match systems, and to modernize, are guaranteed by the treaty. To date, the administration has not yet been clear with regard to how it would structure our forces during the next 6 years, prior to the time when the United States must be "at or below" Article II limits.

Question. Why would this administration need to contemplate or even to complete lower numbers of strategic offensive arms than the limits in New START permit at any time before the treaty itself requires it?

Answer. The long-term goal of U.S. policy is the complete elimination of nuclear weapons. The 2010 Nuclear Posture Review Report stated that the administration would engage Russia after ratification and entry into force of the New START Treaty in negotiations aimed at achieving substantial further nuclear force reductions and transparency that would cover all nuclear weapons—deployed and nondeployed, strategic and nonstrategic.

However, as stated in the NPR, the United States will continue to ensure that, in the calculations of any potential opponent, the perceived gains of attacking the United States or its allies and partners would be far outweighed by the unacceptable costs of the response. The NPR also stated that the size and pace of any future U.S. nuclear force reductions will be implemented in ways that maintain the reliability and effectiveness of our security assurance to our allies and partners.

Question. If it was the administration's intention to "go lower," then why did it not simply extend the START I Treaty, and negotiate a treaty covering deployed, nondeployed and nonstrategic systems as the follow-on to START I?

Answer. The Russian Federation advised the United States that it was not inclined to extend the START Treaty in its current form and wanted a new bilateral treaty. In October 2006, the United States concurred that the START Treaty should not be extended, although some provisions of that Treaty might be carried forward. Thus, a simple extension of the START Treaty was not a viable option, and, in order to reestablish a verification regime, the administration adopted the goal of concluding a new treaty to replace the START Treaty, thus limited to strategic warheads and delivery systems.

48

RESPONSES OF NNSA ADMINISTRATOR D'AGOSTINO TO QUESTIONS
SUBMITTED BY SENATOR RICHARD G. LUGAR

UPLOAD UNDER LOWER NUMBERS

Former Chairman of the Joint Chiefs of Staff Admiral Mullen stated in answers to my questions in 2010 that:

New START . . . provides the United States with the flexibility to deploy, maintain, and modernize its strategic nuclear forces in the manner that best protects U.S. national security interests. The U.S. will retain the ability to "upload" a significant number of nuclear warheads as a hedge against any future technical problems with U.S. delivery platforms or warheads, a technical breakthrough by an adversary that threatens to neutralize a U.S. strategic delivery system, or as a result of a fundamental deterioration in the international security environment.

A recent press article I submit for the record states that an "[administration] official floated the possibility of reducing the number to about 1,000" and that "The United States would also explore the possibility for unilaterally abandoning a portion of [its] roughly 3,000 reserve warheads."

(STORY FOLLOWS)

U.S. TO UNVEIL NEW PLANS TO FURTHER REDUCE NUCLEAR ARSENAL—WASHINGTON, JUNE 16, KYODO NEWS

(HTTP://ENGLISH.KYODONEWS.JP/NEWS/2012/06/164247.HTML)

U.S. President Barack Obama is slated to compile and unveil soon, possibly by the end of this month, plans to further reduce the country's nuclear arsenal, high-level U.S. officials said Friday.

The U.S. government would seek, through future negotiations with Russia, a substantially larger reduction in operational strategic nuclear weapons from the 1,550 the United States is allowed to maintain under a new START treaty with Moscow.

The United States would also explore the possibility for unilaterally abandoning a portion of the roughly 3,000 reserve warheads not yet deployed, the officials said.

While the Obama administration is making final adjustments over the size of the reduction target for operational strategic nuclear weapons, one official floated the possibility of reducing the number to about 1,000. Nuclear experts close to the Obama administration have put the figure at between 1,000 and 1,100. The administration's plans to seek additional cuts in nuclear weapons reflects Obama's aspiration to seek a world without nuclear weapons as proclaimed in a speech in Prague, the Czech Republic, in April 2009.

But the administration plans to make no unilateral cuts in strategic nuclear weapons, instead seeking reassurances from Moscow through a new treaty or a political agreement that Russia would make similar reductions, the officials said. Russia, for its part, is warily watching its Cold War adversary over concern that U.S. efforts to build an antiballistic shield in Europe could render Russia's strategic nuclear weapons ineffective, showing no sign that it would be willing to respond to a U.S. offer. Obama's new operational guidelines for nuclear weapons would be the culmination of work launched after his administration concluded the so-called Nuclear Posture Review in 2010.

The Obama administration has argued that one of the principal roles nuclear weapons play in U.S. policy is to provide a so-called "nuclear umbrella" to such U.S. allies as Japan and South Korea. The administration concluded in its latest review that the United States can maintain an effective nuclear deterrent even if it maintains fewer than the 1,550 strategic nuclear weapons stipulated under the New Strategic Arms Reduction Treaty with Russia, according to the officials. The option of reducing them to the 300 level was discussed but eventually dismissed as insufficient to maintain a credible deterrent, the officials said. The United States currently has about 5,000 nuclear weapons in its stockpile, of which just below 2,000 are operational strategic nuclear weapons, 200 are shorter-range operational tactical weapons, and about 3,000 reserve nuclear warheads. Separately, it has about 3,000 warheads waiting to be dismantled.

Question. Can the United States maintain sufficient and credible upload capability that serves as a hedge against technical and geopolitical uncertainties if it pursues unilateral cuts outside of any treaty?

Answer. NNSA stands ready to support a safe, secure, and effective nuclear arsenal. NNSA is working closely with DOD to ensure requirements and a responsive infrastructure is properly resourced. The Department of Defense and State should address specific questions regarding upload capability, hedge quantities, and treaty implications.

Question. Can NNSA actually support existing Lifetime Extension Programs as well as a large increase in the number of warheads that the United States would eliminate, should deep cuts to the nondeployed hedge be directed?

Answer. Yes, NNSA is planning to support the necessary Life Extension Programs and is working closely with DOD to ensure sufficient resources exist to meet LEP requirements. Cuts to the nondeployed hedge would increase the inventory of weapons awaiting dismantlement. In such a case, NNSA would hold to the commitment to eliminate by FY 2022 the inventory of weapons awaiting dismantlement at the end of FY 2009 and develop an updated plan to eliminate any additional weapons in a safe and fiscally responsible manner.

Question. If so, what are the likely budgetary implications for the NNSA?

Answer. NNSA is currently working closely with the DOD to develop a budget to support the weapons programs. When that effort completes, we will be able to provide a better assessment of the budget implications.

MODERNIZATION COMMITMENTS

The 2010 deal worked out between the administration and the Senate to secure Senate support for ratification of the New START Treaty appears to have fallen apart. The spending reductions in fiscal year 2012 along with those proposed for FY 2013 through FY 2017 for Weapons Activities, erase the $4.1 billion funding increase promised in November 2010. On December 1, 2010, the Directors of the three national nuclear weapons laboratories wrote to me and Chairman Kerry that "We believe that the proposed budgets provide adequate support to sustain the safety, security, reliability, and effectiveness of America's nuclear deterrent within the limit of 1,550 deployed strategic warheads established by the New START Treaty with adequate confidence and acceptable risk."

Question. Given the cuts we have seen enacted to 2010 plans, do you believe that existing and projected budgets for the next five years still provide adequate support to sustain the safety, security, reliability and effectiveness of America's nuclear deterrent within the limit of 1,550 deployed strategic warheads established by the New START Treaty with adequate confidence and acceptable risk?

Answer. The President's budget for 2013 sustains the safety, security, and effectiveness of America's nuclear deterrent.

Congressional appropriations for nuclear weapons in fiscal year 2012 were approximately $416 million less than the President's budget request and fail to meet the resource requirements set forth in the President's 10-year plan, referred to in section 1251 of the National Defense Authorization Act for fiscal year (FY) 2010 (Public Law 111–84; 123 Stat. 2549).

As a result of this shortfall and the constraints of the Budget Control Act of 2011 (Public Law 112–25), enacted in August 2011, the administration is adjusting the 10-year nuclear weapons program. Over the next few months, the Departments of Defense and Energy will continue to work together to develop a responsible and executable plan that ensures the continuation of required programs and capabilities. This will be accomplished while also meeting the new requirements of the Budget Control Act. The Departments are jointly conducting a thorough analysis to ensure that critical capabilities are available when needed, that programs are affordable, and that tradeoffs within the programs are rigorously analyzed.

Question. If so, why?

Answer. The FY 2013 President's budget is the third consecutive increase in the Weapons Activities budget, resulting in a 19-percent increase for Weapons Activities since the FY 2010 budget. That reflects continued support from both the administration and the Congress at a time when there is significant scrutiny of all budgets.

Question. Why has the administration not yet submitted/completed a Future Years Nuclear Security Plan (FYNSP)?

Answer. The administration is committed to ensuring that the nuclear weapons deterrent remains safe, secure, and effective. The FY 2011 and 2012 President's budget requests and their associated Stockpile Stewardship and Management Plans comprehensively addressed the aging stockpile and infrastructure problems head-on.

Under the Budget Control Act of 2011, with new cost estimates for several NNSA programs, and with the $416 million reduction to NNSA's FY 2012 request for weapons activities in the FY 2012 appropriation, the NNSA now faces new fiscal realities. In light of these, NNSA is working with the Department of Defense to conduct the analysis necessary to develop a responsible plan that ensures the continuation of required programs and capabilities, while taking account of these new fiscal realities. This analysis is expected to be completed in time to inform the FY14 budget submission.

CONDITION (9) REPORT

Question. Condition (9) of the December 22, 2010, Senate Resolution of Advice and Consent to the Ratification of the New START treaty required that if appropriations are enacted that fail to meet the resource requirements set forth in the President's 10-year plan, or if at any time more resources are required that estimated in the President' 10-year plan, the President shall submit to Congress within 60 days of such enactment or the identification of the requirement for such additional resources, as appropriate, a report detailing (1) how the President proposed to remedy the resource shortfall; (2) if additional resources are required; (3) the impact of the resource shortfall on the safety, reliability, and performance of United States nuclear forces; and (4) whether and why, in the changed circumstances brought about by the resource shortfall, it remains in the national interest of the United States to remain a Party to the New START Treaty.

We did not receive this report until June of this year, well after 60 days since the enactment of lower levels of appropriations for nuclear weapons in fiscal year 2012.

• Why did it take so long to submit this report?

Answer. Congress passed the Consolidated Appropriations Act, 2012 on December 23, 2011, resulting in an appropriation for Weapons Activities that was $416 million less than requested. At the same time, NNSA, in consultation with our DOD partners, was in the process of finalizing the FY13 President's Budget Request. The appropriation shortfall, and the constraints of the Budget Control Act (Public Law 112–25), necessitated additional adjustments to our programs and delayed our report. As noted in the report you received, we continue to work with DOD to consider the best mix of programs to accomplish DOD priorities within available resources. In addition, NNSA will continue to work to meet these reporting requirements in a timely and accurate manner, and will coordinate with DOD to ensure that this report addresses the concerns expressed by Congress.

ENRICHMENT AND REPROCESSING IN 123 AGREEMENTS

(Answers to the following three questions drafted by the Department of State with DOE/NNSA concurrence)

Earlier this year, the administration adopted a "case-by-case" policy with respect to application of a standard such as may be found in the Agreed Minute to the 2009 123 Agreement with the United Arab Emirates regarding enrichment and reprocessing (ENR). Administration policy is to submit 123 agreements with new countries that do not contain ENR commitments, such as the agreement with Vietnam or Jordan.

Question. Is it true that under the revised Guidelines regarding ENR transfers adopted by the Nuclear Suppliers Group (NSG) that neither Jordan nor Vietnam would qualify for transfers of enrichment technology?

Answer. Under the existing Nuclear Suppliers Group Guidelines, we consider it highly unlikely that any supplier would transfer enrichment technology to either Jordan or Vietnam regardless of whether they meet the criteria. Neither country in the foreseeable future is expected to develop a nuclear power program of sufficient magnitude to justify the establishment of a domestic uranium enrichment capability. If in the future a supplier were to build an enrichment plant in either country, the revised Guidelines rule out the transfer of all technology that could enable the recipient state to replicate it.

Question. If so, then why is the administration apparently no longer seeking ENR commitments from Jordan or Vietnam?

Answer. The administration is currently conducting 123 agreement negotiations with both Jordan and Vietnam. While we are not able to comment publicly on the details of those ongoing negotiations, we are discussing assurances on ENR with both countries.

Question. Will either the Jordan or Vietnam 123 agreements be submitted to Congress this year?

Answer. It is very unlikely that the President will submit any proposed 123 agreements to the Congress in 2012 due to the lack of potential days of continuous session review remaining on the calendar.

EXECUTIVE ORDER REGARDING RUSSIAN HEU

In 1993 the United States agreed to purchase low enriched uranium from the down-blending of 500 metric tons of Russian highly enrichment uranium (HEU). This deal expires in 2013. Russia possesses large amounts of enrichment capacity from its cold war weapons complex. It has half of the world's enrichment capacity and only 7 percent of the world's reactors. On June 25, the President signed an Executive order, and submitted the text of a letter to the Speaker of the House of Representatives and the President of the Senate, both regarding Russian HEU.

Question. What was the necessity for this Executive order?

Answer. The protection of Russian assets in the United States related to the HEU Purchase Agreement was necessitated in 2000. In January 2000, Swiss-based Compagnie Noga D'Importation et D'Exportation S.A. ("Noga") filed suit in the United States to enforce a Swedish arbitration court award against the Russian Federation. Noga sought to seize Russian Federation assets in the United States, including cash payments to the Russian Executive Agent (Techsnabexport or "TENEX") for deliveries made under the HEU Purchase Agreement, as well as the natural uranium hexafluoride component of low enriched uranium (LEU) delivered to Russia under the Agreement.

In May 2000, the Government of the Russian Federation suspended deliveries of LEU derived from Russian weapons-origin HEU under the Purchase Agreement, fearing that future payments for deliveries would be seized in the United States by Noga. The impasse over protection of Russian assets in the United States from Noga and other potential claimants against the Russian Federation threatened to imperil the Agreement and halt the down-blending of Russian HEU from dismantled nuclear weapons.

In June 2000, President Clinton declared a state of national emergency posed by the risk of nuclear proliferation created by the accumulation of large quantities of weapons-usable fissile material in the Russian Federation. The President invoked his International Emergency Economic Powers Act (IEEPA) authority to order all Russian Federation assets in the United States related to the HEU Purchase Agreement protected, and therefore not subject to seizure, attachment, judgment, garnishment, or other judicial process. This protection allowed the Russian Federation to resume shipment of LEU to the United States under the Agreement. Executive Order (EO) 13159 was signed on June 21, 2000.

Each year since 2000, the President has ordered the continuation of the state of national emergency and has renewed EO 13159, thereby protecting Russian assets related to the HEU Purchase Agreement in the United States. Deliveries of LEU derived from nuclear weapons have continued without interruption since 2000. The President's Executive Order 13617 of June 25, 2012, was the most recent order to renew EO 13159 protection and ensure the continuation of the HEU Purchase Agreement for its nonproliferation and international security benefit.

Question. My friend and colleague former Senator Pete Domenici authored legislation in 2008 that links increased Russian access to the U.S. market for enriched uranium with the continued elimination of surplus HEU from Russia's weapons stockpile. What measures are in place to continue our efforts in this regard?

Answer. The United States has demonstrated a desire to down-blend additional Russian HEU beyond 2013, but Russia has expressed no interest in availing itself of the additional U.S. market access offered by Public Law 110–329, also known as the "Domenici Law," in exchange for additional surplus HEU elimination. Russia has declined to consider alternative concepts for continued HEU elimination after the conclusion of the HEU Purchase Agreement, stating that Russia will focus instead on the commercial aspects of exporting LEU and other nuclear services. The United States continues to press Russia on the possibilities for additional Russian HEU down-blending.

Question. After the expiration of the HEU Purchase Agreement (HEUP) next year, is this administration committed to ensuring that if Russia either does not complete the terms of the HEUP or it seeks to increase its market share of U.S. enrichment above 20 to 25 percent, that market access be contingent on continuing nonproliferation efforts to down-blend excess Russian HEU?

Answer. The administration is committed to enforcing both the Agreement Suspending the Antidumping Investigation on Uranium From the Russian Federation and the Domenici Law. This will ensure that if Russia does not complete the terms of the HEU Purchase Agreement or seeks to increase Russia's share of the U.S. enriched uranium market to more than 20 percent during the 2014–2020 time period, market access will be contingent on the further elimination of Russian HEU.

————

RESPONSES OF NNSA ADMINISTRATOR THOMAS P. D'AGOSTINO TO QUESTIONS
SUBMITTED BY SENATOR TOM UDALL

Question. Has NNSA made the right decision with regards to its responsibility to maintain critical infrastructure and ensure that our most critical resources, our people who do the work at the labs, are taken care of? The existing CMR facility, completed in 1952, resides on a seismic fault. This fact has led to the closure of one wing, and the scaling down of work in the facility. Much of the infrastructure at the current CMR facility is outdated and/or not up to current standards for safety and scientific research. According to conclusions in the bipartisan report "America's Strategic Posture: Final Report of the Congressional Commission on the Strategic Posture of the United States" (Strategic Posture Report), the site is "genuinely decrepit and . . . maintained in a safe and secure manner only at high cost." NNSA has continually mismanaged and delayed the replacement project, and I hope that the Congress can find a solution, which will benefit our national security by investing in our scientific base and ensuring that we have the tools to meet critical mission requirements.

Not since 2008 has Los Alamos National Labs been forced to make serious cuts to its workforce. In February of this year, Director Charles McMillan, in an attempt to save money as a result of budget shortfalls, primarily in weapons funding, announced that LANL would make cuts in its workforces by seeking voluntary retirements between 400 and 800 personnel.

- Has NNSA assessed how these cuts will impact the technical and scientific expertise at the labs, and the ability of LANL to both maintain and recruit the talented staff it needs to maintain its scientific and national security mission?

Answer. Maintaining the vitality of the scientific and technical workforce is assessed at the overall laboratory level. Two areas continue to be important: the retention of our most critical, and difficult to reconstitute, skills and the future ability to draw talent into the laboratory. LANS implemented a voluntary separation program this year and accepted 557 applicants. Prior to accepting applications, LANS assessed their skills and determined they were not critical to mission accomplishment. If an applicant possessed critical skills, they were not allowed to participate in the program. During the process, LANS assured NNSA they would be able to continue to provide world-class science and meet mission requirements. In addition, we are streamlining Laboratory Directed Research and Development (LDRD) approvals that help foster innovation, continuing strategic discussions among interagency leadership on the critical skills needed to support the Nation's broader national security interests through our four-agency Governance Charter, and focusing on the next generation through pipeline programs, including minority serving institutions. As NNSA continues to study the impacts to existing facilities, personnel, and Nuclear Security Enterprise capabilities, workforce plans will be adjusted as necessary to meet mission requirements. In addition, the National Academy study on the quality of science at the NNSA laboratories, including Los Alamos, will provide us with a valuable external assessment.

Question. And has NNSA determined or studied the impact on recruitment, retention, and training of the critical and highly talented Los Alamos workforce if the CMR is closed in 2019 without CMRR–NF built to replace it and how will the delay of CMRR–NF impact the overall scientific mission at the labs?

Answer. NNSA and the laboratory work closely together to ensure all appropriate steps are taken to effectively recruit, retain, and train the Los Alamos workforce. Deferral of CMRR–NF construction for at least 5 years has had an immediate effect on the temporary construction workforce that was planned to construct CMRR–NF. A plan is being finalized to maintain continuity in analytical chemistry and material characterization capabilities by leveraging existing LANL facilities as we continue the transition out of CMR. As a result, we do not expect the planned completion of transitioning NNSA program operations from CMR to other facilities by approximately 2019 to have a major effect on the laboratory's plutonium workforce.

Question. Given the importance of maintaining the intellectual capability at Los Alamos, which as the 2009 Strategic Posture Report stated was "in immediate danger of attrition" because there is a risk that the "broad, diverse, and deep set of scientific skills . . ." could be lost if NNSA did not build the CMRR–NF facility.

And, because the degradation of critical infrastructure at LANL not only impacts the nuclear mission, but also other national security priorities such as nonproliferation, nuclear threat reduction, nuclear forensics, alternative energy programs, and other highly technical programs.

- Why did NNSA make the decision to completely zero out the program without, as the SASC mark has concluded, seeking input from the labs, Congress, and DOD, and without analyzing the long-term impact on our intellectual infrastructure?

Answer. NNSA considered input from the Laboratory Directors and coordinated with DOD; the Secretary consulted several independent sets of advisors; and NNSA used the direction and guidance in the markup of the FY 2012 Congressional Budget process to inform the development of the President's Budget Request for FY 2013. There was broad consensus on the direction that was adopted. During budget formulation when the President's budget data had to be embargoed, NNSA officials continued to meet with congressional staff as requested. Throughout this process, NNSA received expert advice from the labs and plants. Through these consultations and analyses, we began to have concerns about our ability to simultaneously execute two construction projects estimated at $4–7 billion each (namely UPF and CMRR–NF), especially given the fiscal realities of the Budget Control Act and reductions to the President's FY 2012 budget. Following a series of meetings between DOD and DOE officials, the Nuclear Weapons Council signed out a letter on March 27, 2012, acknowledging the programmatic realignments including the decision to defer construction of CMRR–NF for at least 5 years.

This decision was made conscious of the fact that deferring CMRR–NF would increase long-term risk to the overall mission, specifically, risk associated with the need to achieve a responsive, resilient infrastructure, which extends beyond the needs of the currently scheduled LEPs. NNSA, DOD and the Laboratory Directors believe that the interim strategy presents an acceptable, short-term level of risk to our plutonium capabilities, while protecting the core elements of the program including the intellectual infrastructure.

Question. The fiscal year 2012 DOE budget predicted a need of $190 million for the Y–12 UPF project in fiscal year 2013, and $350 million in 2014. CMRR–NF, according to the fiscal year 2012 submission would require $300 million in 2013 and $350 million in 2014. In the fiscal year 2013 budget submission those numbers were very different. Instead of $190 million for UPF, the request was increased to $340 million, a $150 million plus up. On the other hand, CMRR–NF was reduced to zero. The SASC mark authorizes $150 million of the amounts appropriated in fiscal year 2013 for the construction of the CMRR–NF facility and prohibits NNSA from reducing amounts authorized for UPF.

- Why did NNSA determine there was a need to plus-up UPF by $150 million just a year after NNSA proposed a smaller need?

Answer. Given the fiscal realities of the Budget Control Act, NNSA studied alternatives to continue meeting the mission and determined that construction of the Uranium Processing Facility (UPF) Project, the B61–12 Life Extension Program (LEP), and construction of the CMRR–NF Project could not continue simultaneously. The decision to move forward with UPF construction and the B61–12 LEP, but defer CMRR nuclear facility construction, was made after consultation with Laboratory Directors and Nuclear Weapons Council members, and is fully consistent with findings from an independent DOD review of both projects in 2011 that confirmed Building 9212 at Y–12 presents the highest programmatic and operational risk. In order to address the greatest risks and to implement lessons learned from other projects regarding the benefits of a front-loaded budget profile, NNSA requested accelerated funding for the UPF Project and revised the UPF project plan to prioritize the replacement of the highest-risk operations in Building 9212.

Question. Los Alamos Director Charles McMillan testified in April regarding the cost of CMRR–NF that "Our current estimate at Los Alamos is something in the region of $3.7 billion, but . . . as delay occurs, we are moving toward . . . $5 billion." Former Director Anastasio also testified previously that "any delay in a project ultimately costs you money. So, if we delay the start and the process of this facility, it means, in the end, the integrated costs—although in 1 year you might save money, over the life of the project, it's going to cost you money."

Given this testimony, wouldn't it be more prudent, as stewards of taxpayer dollars, to fund CMRR–NF at a lower level than proposed, perhaps at $150 million as the SASC mark proposes? This might require a more equitable sharing of the burdens across the labs, but could prevent delays in the project and prevent what Los Alamos Director McMillan said could drastically increase the price of the building . . . while also protecting our intellectual base.

Answer. CMRR–NF was deferred to allow NNSA to pursue higher priority and more urgent stockpile management commitments, while continuing to meet DOD's plutonium requirements and sustaining our existing infrastructure and key science, technology, and engineering programs. Any other requirements or activities deferred or delayed, in lieu of deferring CMRR–NF, would be subject to a similar escalation in cost. However, NNSA considers the deferral of CMRR–NF as the option that introduces the least additional risk to the overall program.

Question. Did NNSA consider cutting other less vital programs instead of CMRR–NF and which programs were considered?

Answer. NNSA analyzed alternatives other than deferring CMRR–NF. The three other options identified were to (1) defer construction of the Uranium Processing Facility (UPF), (2) significantly reduce Facilities Operations and Maintenance, or (3) in consultation with DOD, reduce the scope of the B61–12 LEP. NNSA assessed that underfunding facility maintenance would have put all the prioritized activities of our core capabilities at an unacceptable risk level. NNSA also determined that a deferral of UPF would be unacceptable, because it would require NNSA to conduct stockpile modernization in a facility with an increasingly high risk of significant shutdown and for which there were no viable alternatives. In addition, reducing B61–12 LEP scope beyond DOD threshold requirements would adversely affect the nuclear deterrent.

Question. The 2009 Congressional Commission on the Strategic Posture of the United States found that "a short-term loss of plutonium capabilities may hurt the weapon program more than a short-term loss of enriched uranium capabilities." Furthermore, the Strategic Posture Report also found that the "Los Alamos plutonium facility is required independent of stockpile size" and that "the Los Alamos facility has the more mature design."

- Given this finding, why has NNSA decided to move ahead with the Y–12 Uranium Processing Facility ahead of the CMRR–NF facility at Los Alamos instead of concurrently as originally planned?

Answer. In a time of fiscal austerity, NNSA is committed to being a responsible steward of taxpayer dollars. The decision to move forward with UPF construction and defer CMRR nuclear facility construction was made after extended consultation with our Laboratory Directors and the Nuclear Weapons Council members, and is fully consistent with findings from an independent DOD review of both projects in 2011 that confirmed Building 9212 at Y–12 presents the highest programmatic and operational risk. Given the not less than 5-year deferral of CMRR–NF construction, NNSA is preparing to take steps with an interim plutonium strategy to ensure continuity of all required capabilities and uninterrupted plutonium operations.

Question. The Lab Directors and Department of Defense have been clear that the current NNSA plan does not meet critical national defense mission requirements. This seems to contradict NNSA's assertion in its Revised Plutonium Strategy-Supplemental Information for the President's FY 2013 Budget Request that "With the delay in CMRR–NF construction, NNSA will maintain the Nation's plutonium capability using existing infrastructure and capabilities." Furthermore, the November 2010 Update to the National Defense Authorization Act of FY 2010 Section 1251 Report (1251 Report) stated that both CMRR and UPF Construction are "required to ensure the United States can maintain a safe, secure, and effective arsenal over the long-term" and that the "Administration remains committed to their construction."

- How does delaying the construction of CMRR meet that commitment and does NNSA disagree with the testimony by the current and former Directors, and the Department of Defense, that Los Alamos and NNSA do not have the capability to meet mission requirements without the construction of CMRR–NF?

Answer. The need for the long-term capabilities of CMRR–NF is still valid and will be addressed. Although it does increase risk to the mission, deferring CMRR–NF construction for at least 5 years will enable NNSA to meet higher priority and

more urgent near term commitments, including stockpile assessment and maintenance, W76–1 LEP, B61–12 LEP, W88 Alt 370, and UPF. The short-term risks associated with deferring CMRR–NF were assessed by NNSA, the Laboratory Directors
and the Department of Defense to be manageable, with near term planning and production adjustments, which can provide sufficient production capacity (for approximately 30 newly manufactured pits/year and 90 reused pits/year starting in
FY2021) to meet stockpile commitments over the subsequent decade. A portion of
this mission risk, which does represent a change from prior statements and assessments, will be mitigated by a recent change consistent with international standards
that allows significantly more plutonium to be handled and processed at the Radiological Laboratory Utility/Office Building (RLUOB) than previously had been projected when construction of the RLUOB was completed. In addition, with advanced
planning and production, that level of capability does not preclude consideration of
remanufacturing pits for upcoming life extension efforts. This production rate is less
than the 50–80pits/year that CMRR–NF would have enabled, and NNSA projects
that the higher production level is not required until the early 2030s. As such, the
lower production rate of 30 pits/year, plus the availability of existing off-the-shelf
pits, allows NNSA to provide the pits we need on the schedule approved by the
Nuclear Weapons Council for at least the next decade. As part of the ongoing
NNSA–DOD analysis, we are developing an enduring, long-term plutonium capability to provide a higher sustained rate of pit manufacturing ahead of the projected
need in the 2030s . . . Key DOD officials and one laboratory Director endorsed the
interim and enduring plutonium plan during the August 1 meeting with six
Senators.

Question. You mentioned in your exchange with Senator Corker that changes at
RLUOB could handle the required production levels to meet DOD's mission requirements absent CMRR–NF. However, NNSA's 60 day report found that Los Alamos
could only meet less than half of the minimum DOD mission requirements with
extra shift work, and that increasing capabilities by just a small margin would take
investment in other lab facilities to do the analytical chemistry and materials characterization, plus a 5-year study of reuse capability that may likely find that reuse
is not an option. How then did NNSA conclude that there is a plan to meet mission
requirements since NNSA's best plan is incomplete and why, therefore, did NNSA
choose to delay CMRR–NF knowing that there was not a suitable alternative which
met DOD mission requirements as outlined in the 2010 Memo of Agreement
between DOD and the Department of Energy?

Answer. During at least the next 5-year period of deferral for CMRR–NF construction, NNSA plans to meet future DOD stockpile requirements through a combination of capabilities found at Los Alamos and other sites. For example, the recently
constructed Radiological Laboratory/Utility/Office Building (RLUOB) has been authorized to work with larger quantities of plutonium, consistent with international
standards, and will provide the opportunity to install additional equipment in
RLUOB to optimize analytical chemistry capabilities. NNSA and Los Alamos are
also evaluating the availability and adequacy of specific support capabilities at several other sites, so that the integrated set of national capabilities will be identified
and prepared to support pit production. In sum, the interim plutonium strategy will
assure that we will get the pits we need on the schedule the Nuclear Weapons
Council—chaired by DOD and NNSA—has determined is necessary.

With a planned production rate of ~30 newly manufactured pits/year plus ~90
reuse pits/year, the interim plutonium strategy will support upcoming LEPs with
a combination of remanufactured and reused pits. There are technical hurdles to be
overcome with regard to pit reuse, but the laboratories and NNSA are cautiously
optimistic we will be able to successfully resolve them. While this approach does increase risk, DOD and NNSA agreed that this risk was manageable, and we would
still be able to meet DOD requirements.

○

www.ingramcontent.com/pod-product-compliance
Lightning Source LLC
Chambersburg PA
CBHW080546290526
45790CB00006B/2576